BIRDS OF ASIA & AUSTRALIA

AN ILLUSTRATED ENCYCLOPEDIA AND BIRDWATCHING GUIDE

DAVID ALDERTON

southwater

This edition is published by Southwater

Southwater is an imprint of Anness Publishing Ltd
Hermes House, 88–89 Blackfriars Road, London SE1 8HA
tel. 020 7401 2077; fax 020 7633 9499
www.southwaterbooks.com; info@anness.com

UK agent: The Manning Partnership Ltd; tel. 01225 478444;
fax 01225 478440; sales@manning-partnership.co.uk
UK distributor: Grantham Book Services Ltd; tel. 01476 541080;
fax 01476 541061; orders@gbs.tbs-ltd.co.uk
North American agent/distributor: National Book Network; tel. 301 459 3366;
fax 301 429 5746; www.nbnbooks.com
Australian agent/distributor: Pan Macmillan Australia; tel. 1300 135 113; fax 1300 135 103;
customer.service@macmillan.com.au
New Zealand agent/distributor: David Bateman Ltd; tel. (09) 415 7664; fax (09) 415 8892

Publisher: Joanna Lorenz
Editorial Director: Helen Sudell
Project Editors: Debra Mayhew and Catherine Stuart
Designer: Nigel Partridge
Illustrators: see picture acknowledgements, below
Production Controller: Darren Price

Previously published as part of a larger volume, *The World Encyclopedia of
Birds & Birdwatching*

1 3 5 7 9 10 8 6 4 2

PICTURE ACKNOWLEDGEMENTS

Illustrations appearing on pages 1–5: page 1, cockatiels *(Nymphicus hollandicus)*;
page 2, red-rumped parrots *(Psephotus haematonotus)*; page 3, java sparrows
(Londchura oryzivora); page 4t, green broadbills *(Calyptomena viridis)*; page 4b, black-billed
sicklebill (Drepanornis albertisii); page 5t, rainbow lorikeet *(Trichoglossus haematodus)*;
page 5b, glossy ibis *(Plengadis falcinellus)*

Thanks to the following for permission to
reproduce their photographs in this book.
Key: l = left, r = right, t = top,
m = middle, b = bottom

David Alderton: 6–7, 11mr, 11br, 14t, 17b,
19bl, 19br, 20bl, 21b, 21tr, 26bl, 27t, 27b,
29t, 29m, 29b, 30t, 31t, 33t, 33b, 35t, 35m.
Dennis Avon: Jacket, 2, 11tl, 11tr, 11ml,
13tl, 13mr, 15t, 21tl, 24br, 26tm, 30t, 31m,
31b, 32t, 32b, 35b, 36t, 36b, 37t, 37b.

Ardea: 12r, 13b, 17m, 18, 22b, 23b, 24t,
25t, 26b, 30b, 34t, 39l, 39m, 39r.
Oxford Scientific Films: 9, 12l, 15ml, 16t,
16b, 22t, 23tl, 23tr, 24bl, 25b, 28t.

Illustrations were provided by:

Peter Barrett: 40, 41, 44, 45, 46, 48, 49,
50, 52–69, 81, 82, 88.
Anthony Duke: 42, all location maps,
pp41–93.

Martin Knowelden: 8–9, 10, 15, 17,
19, 20, 26, 28.
Andrew Robinson: 86, 87, 92, 93.
Tim Thackeray: 11, 42, 43, 46, 47, 48
50, 51, 70–85, 88–91.

CONTENTS

UNDERSTANDING BIRDS

The most obvious thing that distinguishes all birds, from a tiny red-breasted pygmy parrot (*Micropsitta bruijnii*) to a giant, double-wattled cassowary (*Casuarius casuarius*), is the presence of feathers on their bodies. The need for birds to be light in weight, so that they can fly with minimum effort, has led to significant, evolutionary changes within their bodies, yet the basic skeletal structure of all birds is remarkably similar, irrespective of their size. In other words, birds are unmistakable. It is clear that even the few groups of flightless birds, such as penguins (Spheniscidae), are descended from ancestors that possessed the power of flight, although these birds have since evolved along different lines to suit their habitat.

The other feature unique to birds is that all species reproduce by means of calcareous eggs. However, birds' breeding habits are very diverse. Some birds even transfer the task of incubation to other species, by laying eggs in their nests, while others create natural incubators that serve to hatch their chicks and carefully regulate the temperature inside.

There is even greater diversity in the feeding habits of birds, as reflected by differences in their bill structure, and also their digestive tract. Birds' dietary preferences play a critical part in the environment as well. For example, in tropical rainforests, many fruit-eating species help to disperse indigestible seeds through the forest, thus helping to ensure the natural regeneration of the vegetation.

The birds of tropical rainforests are often surprisingly hard to observe, betraying their presence more by their calls than by their bright colours. However, birds can be easily observed in many other localities. Birdwatching itself can develop into an absorbing pastime offering an unparalleled insight into the natural world. A wide range of accessories is now available for an ever-growing number of enthusiasts, from close-range viewing equipment to specialist clothing, which can be easily obtained via magazines and websites.

The second part of this book contains a directory of over 100 birds living in Asia and Australia. The detailed colour artworks and profiles of distribution, size, habitat, eggs and food will help you to recognize a host of different birds, both in your neighbourhood and further afield.

Left: Many birds, such as these Australian rainbow lorikeets (*Trichoglossus haematodus*), live socially in flocks. Group living brings these birds distinct survival benefits, the most obvious being increased protection from predators.

THE ORIGINS OF BIRDS

Vertebrates – first flying reptiles called pterosaurs, and later birds – took to the air about 190 million years ago. Adapting to an aerial existence marked a very significant step in vertebrate development, because of the need for a new method of locomotion, and a radically different body design.

The age of *Archaeopteryx*

Back in 1861, workers in a limestone quarry in Bavaria, southern Germany, unearthed a strange fossil that resembled a bird in appearance and was about the size of a modern crow, but also had teeth. The idea that the fossil was a bird was confirmed by the clear evidence of feathers impressed into the stone, as the presence of plumage is one of the characteristic distinguishing features of all birds. The 1860s were a time when the debate surrounding evolution was becoming fierce, and the discovery created huge interest, partly because it suggested that birds may have evolved from dinosaurs. It confirmed that birds had lived on Earth for at least 145 million years, existing even before the age of the dinosaurs came to a close in the Cretaceous period, about 65 million years ago. As the oldest known bird, it was given the name *Archaeopteryx*, meaning "ancient wings".

Pterosaurs

A study of the anatomy of *Archaeopteryx*'s wings revealed that these early birds did not just glide but were capable of using their wings for active flight. Yet they were not the first vertebrate creatures to have taken to the skies. The pterosaurs had already successfully developed approximately 190 million years ago, during the Jurassic period, and even shared the skies with birds for a time. In fact, remains of one of the later pterosaurs, called *Rhamphorhynchus*, have been found in the same limestone deposits in southern Germany where *Archaeopteryx* was discovered. The pterosaur's wings more closely resembled those of a bat than a bird, consisting simply of a membrane supported by a bony framework, rather than feathers overlying the skin.

Some types of pterosaurs developed huge wingspans, in excess of 7m (23ft), which enabled them to glide almost effortlessly over the surface of the world's oceans, much like albatrosses do today. It appears that they fed primarily on fish and other marine life, scooping their food out of the water in flight. Changes in climate probably doomed the pterosaurs, however, since increasingly turbulent weather patterns meant that gliding became difficult, and they could no longer fly with ease.

Avian giants

In the period immediately after the extinction of the dinosaurs, some groups of birds increased rapidly in physical size, and in so doing, lost the ability to fly. Since their increased size meant that they could cover large distances on foot, and as they faced no predators because large hunting mammals had not yet evolved, these large birds were relatively safe. In New Zealand, home of the large flightless moas, such giants thrived until the start of human settlement about a millennium ago. The exact date of the final extinction of the moas is not recorded, but the group had probably died out entirely by the middle of the 19th century.

Above: An impression of how Archaeopteryx *may have looked. It is impossible to be sure of its coloration from its fossilized remains.*

Below: The largest species of moa would have dwarfed a man.

Below: All pterosaurs had a similar body shape with a narrow head, which may have been embellished with a crest of some sort. This may have been used for display purposes and also to reduce air resistance in flight. The wing structure of pterosaurs was very different from that of birds: their wings basically consisted of skin membranes, stretched out behind the forearms.

It was this large surface area that allowed them to glide with little effort, but becoming airborne in the first place required great effort. The lack of body covering over the skin also had the effect of causing greater heat loss from the body. In birds, the feathers provide insulation as well as assisting active flight.

Below: Hoatzin chicks (Opisthocomus hoazin) are unique among today's birds in possessing claws on their wing tips, which help them to climb trees. The claws are lost by the time the birds are old enough to fly.

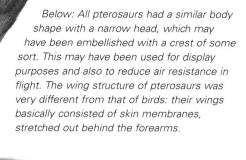

The spread of birds

After the age of *Archaeopteryx*, it is thought that birds continued to radiate out over the globe and became increasingly specialized. Unfortunately, there is very little fossil evidence to help us understand their early history. This lack of fossils is partly due to the fact that the small carcasses of birds would have been eaten whole by scavengers, and partly because their lightweight, fragile skeletons would not have fossilized easily. In addition, most birds would not have been trapped and died under conditions that were favourable for fossilization.

By the end of the age of the dinosaurs, birds had become far more numerous. Many seabirds still possessed teeth in their jaws, reflecting their reptilian origins. These probably assisted them in catching fish and other aquatic creatures. It was at this stage that the ancestors of contemporary bird groups such as waterfowl and gulls started to emerge. Most of the forerunners of today's birds had evolved by the Oligocene epoch, some 38 million years ago.

Some groups of birds that existed in these times have since disappeared, notably the phororhacids, which ranged widely over South America and even into parts of the southern United States. These birds were fearsome predators, capable of growing to nearly 3m (10ft) in height. They were equipped with deadly beaks and talons, and probably hunted together in groups.

Recent finds

During the mid-1990s, the discovery of avian fossils in China that were apparently contemporary with those of *Archaeopteryx* aroused considerable interest. Like its German relative, *Confuciusornis* possessed claws on the tips of its wings, which probably helped these early birds to move around. Similar claws are seen today in hoatzin chicks. *Confuciusornis* resembled modern birds more closely than *Archaeopteryx* in one significant respect: it lacked teeth in its jaws. Further study of the recent fossil finds from this part of the world is required, however, as some may not be genuine.

THE SKELETON AND PARTS OF A BIRD

The bird's skeleton has evolved to be light yet robust, both characteristics that help with flight. To this end, certain bones, particularly in the skull, have become fused, while others are absent, along with the teeth. The result is that birds' bodies are lightweight compared to those of other vertebrates.

In order to be able to fly, a bird needs a lightweight body so that it can become airborne with minimal difficulty. It is not just teeth that are missing from the bird's skull, but the associated heavy jaw muscles as well. These have been replaced by a light, horn-covered bill that is adapted in shape to the bird's feeding habits. Some of the limb bones, such as the humerus in the shoulder, are hollow, which also cuts down on weight. At the rear of the body, the bones in the vertebral column have become fused, which gives greater stability as well as support for the tail feathers.

The avian skeleton

In birds, the greatest degree of specialization is evident in the legs. Their location is critical to enable a bird to maintain its balance. The legs are found close to the midline, set slightly back near the bird's centre of gravity. These limbs are powerful, helping to provide lift at take-off and absorb the impact of landing. Strong legs also allow most birds to hop over the ground with relative ease.

There are some differences in the skeleton between different groups of birds. The atlas and axis bones at the start of the vertebral column are fused in the case of hornbills, for example, but in no other family.

Feet and toes

Birds' feet vary in length, and are noticeably extended in waders, which helps them to distribute their weight more evenly. The four toes may be arranged either in a typical 3:1 perching grip, with three toes gripping the front of the perch and one behind, or in a 2:2 configuration, known as zygodactyl, which gives a surer grip. The zygodactyl grip is seen in relatively few groups of birds, notably parrots and toucans. Touracos have flexible toes so they can swap back and forth between these two options.

The zygodactyl arrangement of their toes helps some parrots to use their feet like hands for holding food. Birds generally have claws at the ends of their toes, which have developed into sharp talons in the case of birds of prey, helping them to catch their quarry even in flight. Many birds also use their claws for preening, and they can provide balance for birds that run or climb.

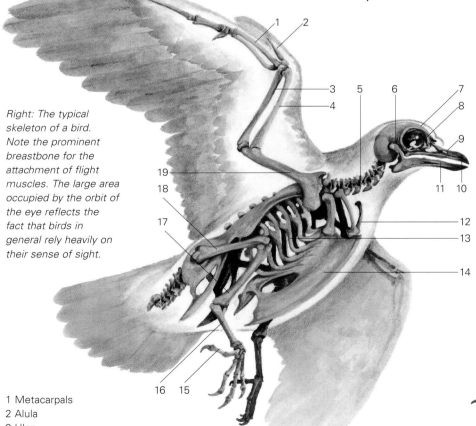

Right: The typical skeleton of a bird. Note the prominent breastbone for the attachment of flight muscles. The large area occupied by the orbit of the eye reflects the fact that birds in general rely heavily on their sense of sight.

Parrot

Above: Parrots use their feet for holding food, in a similar way to human hands.

Bird of prey

Above: In birds of prey, the claws have become talons for grasping prey.

Wader

Above: Long toes make it easier for waders to walk over muddy ground or water plants.

Duck

Above: The webbed feet of ducks provide propulsion in water.

1 Metacarpals
2 Alula
3 Ulna
4 Radius
5 Cervical vertebrae
6 Ear
7 Cranium
8 Eye socket
9 Nostril
10 Bill (upper mandible)
11 Bill (lower mandible)
12 Clavicle (wishbone)
13 Ribs
14 Sternum (breastbone)
15 Metatarsals
16 Tarsus
17 Tibia and Fibula
18 Femur
19 Humerus

Walking across water

Some birds have become extremely specialized in their habits, and their limbs have evolved to work in harmony with their environment. The pheasant-tailed jacana (*Hydrophasianus chirurgus*), a wader of tropical and subtropical marshlands in South-east Asia, is one such example. The very long toes supporting the legs of these birds distribute their weight over a wide area, enabling them to walk nimbly, or perch, on the leaves of aquatic plants without sinking into the water. These shy birds can be seen stepping across waterlilies and lotuses with such ease and elegance that they have earned the Chinese nickname *ling po xian zi*, which translates as "fairies walking over ripples". In addition to its agility above the water, the jacana is also a powerful swimmer, and able to escape danger by diving beneath the surface.

Bills

The bills of birds vary quite widely in shape and size, and reflect their feeding habits. The design of the bill has an impact on the force that it can generate. The bills of many larger parrots are especially strong, allowing them to crack hard nut shells. In addition, they can move their upper and lower bill independently, which produces a wider gape and, in turn, allows more pressure to be exerted. The tongue can also assist feeding. Those of lories and lorikeets have small projections which act rather like brushes, sweeping pollen granules up from flowers.

Above: The narrow, curved bill of spider-hunters (Nectariniidae) enables these birds to probe flowers to extract nectar and insects.

Above: Fire-tufted barbets (Psilopogon pyrolophus) have a stocky bill, often used for beating out a nesting chamber in rotten wood.

Above: This Timor dusky sparrow (Padda fuscata) displays the conical bill shape of most finches, which enables them to crack seeds.

Above: The bill of a penguin (Spheniscidae) must be powerful in order to catch, and hold on to, large fish and other underwater prey.

Above: The curved bill of this Australian king parrot (Alisterus scapularis) is a familiar sight; the pointed upper bill can easily crack seeds.

Above: Hornbills (Bucerotidae) use their prominent bills to pluck fruits and seize vertebrate prey with relative ease.

Wings

A bird's wing is built around just three digits, which correspond to human fingers. In contrast, bats have five digits supporting their fleshy membranes. The three digits of birds provide a highly robust structure.

The power of the wings is further enhanced by the fusion of the carpals and wrist bones to create a single bone known as the carpometacarpus. This runs along the rear of the wing.

At the front of the chest, the clavicles are joined together to form what is often referred to as the 'wishbone' in chickens. The large, keel-shaped breastbone, or sternum, runs along the underside of the body. It is bound by the ribs to the backbone, which provides stability, especially during flight. In addition, birds use their flight muscles, the most powerful of which are the pectorals, to provide the main propulsive thrust when they are airborne.

Right: The pheasant-tailed jacana (Hydrophasianus chirurgus) gets its name from its long, sweeping tail feathers. Other members of this family can be found in the wetlands of Africa and South America, and display similar habits to their Asiatic relatives.

FEATHERS

The presence of feathers is one of the main distinguishing characteristics that set birds apart from other groups of creatures on the planet. The number of feathers on a bird's body varies considerably – a swan may have as many as 25,000 feathers, for instance, while a tiny hummingbird has just 1,000 in all.

Aside from the bill, legs and feet, the entire body of the bird is covered in feathers. The plumage does not grow randomly over the bird's body, but develops along lines of so-called feather tracts, or pterylae. These are separated by bald areas known as apteria. The apteria are not conspicuous under normal circumstances, because the contour feathers overlap to cover the entire surface of the body. Plumage may also sometimes extend down over the legs and feet as well, in the case of birds from cold climates, providing extra insulation here.

Feathers are made of a tough protein called keratin, which is also found in our hair and nails. Birds have three main types of feathers: the body, or contour, feathers; the strong, elongated flight feathers on the wings; and the warm, wispy down feathers next to the bird's skin.

A diet deficient in sulphur-containing amino acids, which are the basic building blocks of protein, will result in poor feathering, creating "nutritional barring" across the flight and tail feathers. Abnormal plumage coloration can also have nutritional causes in some cases. These changes are usually reversible if more favourable environmental conditions precede the next moult.

The functions of feathers

Plumage has a number of functions, not just relating to flight. It provides a barrier that retains warm air close to the bird's body and helps to maintain body temperature, which is higher in birds than mammals – typically between 41 and 43.5°C (106 and 110°F). The down feathering that lies close to the skin, and the overlying contour plumage, are vital for maintaining body warmth. Most birds have a small volume relative to their surface area, which can leave them vulnerable to hypothermia.

A special oil produced by the preen gland, located at the base of the tail, waterproofs the plumage. This oil, which is spread over the feathers as the bird preens itself, prevents water penetrating the feathers, which would cause the bird to become so

Below: Feathering is highly significant for display purposes in some species, particularly members of the Phasanidae family. The cock blue peafowl (Pavo cristatus) has a very elaborate train of feathers, which it fans open to deter rivals and attract mates.

Above: A bird's flight feathers are longer and more rigid than the contour feathers that cover the body, or the fluffy down feathers that lie next to the skin. The longest, or primary, flight feathers, which generate the most thrust, are located along the outer rear edges of the wings. Tail feathers are often similar in shape to the flight feathers, with the longest located in the centre. Splaying the tail feathers increases drag and so slows the bird down.

1 Primaries	9 Auricular region
2 Secondaries	(ear)
3 Axillaries	10 Nape
4 Rump	11 Back
5 Lateral tail feathers	12 Greater under-
6 Central tail feathers	wing coverts
7 Breast	13 Lesser under-
8 Cere	wing coverts

Above: The brilliant coloration of the male crimson sunbird (Aethopyga siparaja) *sets it apart from the female, whose greyish-olive plumage is dull by comparison.*

waterlogged that it could no longer fly. The contour feathers that cover the body are also important for camouflage in many birds. Barring, in particular, breaks up the outline of the bird's body, helping to conceal it in its natural habitat.

The plumage has become modified in some cases, reflecting the individual lifestyle of the species concerned. Woodpeckers, for example, have tail feathers that are short and rather sharp at their tips, providing additional support for gripping on to the sides of trees. Vultures, on the other hand, have bare heads because plumage here would soon become stained and matted with blood when these birds fed on a carcass.

Social significance of plumage

Plumage can also be important in social interactions between birds. Many species have differences in their feathering that separate males from females, and often juveniles can also be distinguished by their plumage. Cock birds are usually more brightly coloured, which helps them to attract their mates, but this does not apply in every case. The difference between the sexes in terms of their plumage can be quite marked. Cock birds of a number of species have feathers forming crests as well as magnificent tail plumes, which are seen to greatest effect in peacocks (*Pavo cristatus*), whose display is one of the most remarkable sights in the whole of the avian world.

Recent studies have confirmed that birds that to our eyes appear relatively dull in colour, such as the hill mynah (*Gracula religiosa*) with its blackish plumage, are seen literally in a different light by other birds. They can visually perceive the ultraviolet component of light, which is normally invisible to us, making these seemingly dull birds appear greener. Ultraviolet coloration may also be significant in helping birds to choose their mates.

Moulting

Birds' feathering is maintained by preening, but it becomes frayed and worn over time. It is therefore replaced by new plumage during the process of moulting, when the old feathers are shed. Moulting is most often an annual event. However, many young birds shed their nest feathers before they are a year old.

Moulting may also be triggered by the onset of the breeding season in some species, as is the case in many whydahs and weavers. These birds resemble sparrows for much of the year, but their appearance is transformed at the onset of the breeding period. Whydah cock birds develop lengthy tail plumes, and the birds also become more strikingly coloured. Hormonal alterations in the body are important in triggering this process, with external factors such as changing day length also playing a part.

Right: The feather shaft holds the feather in place in the skin. The barbs run off the shaft at regular intervals, rather like the branches of a tree, and divide into smaller branches called barbules. These have tiny hooks attached to them that reinforce the structure of the flight feather, making it more rigid.

Barb Barbule

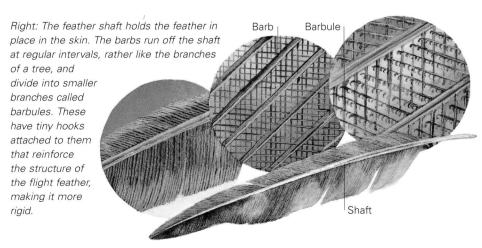

Shaft

FLIGHT

Some birds spend much of their lives in the air, whereas others will only fly as a last resort if threatened. A few species are too heavy to take off at all. The mechanics of flight are similar in all birds, but flight patterns vary significantly, which can help to identify the various groups in the air.

In most cases, the whole structure of the bird's body has evolved to facilitate flight. It is important for a bird's body weight to be relatively light, because this lessens the muscular effort required to keep it airborne. The powerful flight muscles, which provide the necessary lift, can account for up to a third of the bird's total body weight. They are attached to the breastbone, or sternum, in the midline of the body, and run along the sides of the body from the clavicle along the breastbone to the top of the legs.

Weight and flight

There is an upper weight limit of just over 18kg (40lb), above which birds would not be able to take off successfully. Some larger birds, notably pelicans and swans, need a run-up in order to gain sufficient momentum to lift off, particularly from water. Smaller birds can dart straight off a perch. Approaching the critical upper weight limit for flight, the male Australian bustard (*Choriotis australis*) is one of the world's heaviest flying birds, although it prefers to run due to the effort in becoming airborne.

Below: A typical take-off, as demonstrated by this bird of prey. The bird's feet play almost as vital a role as the wings.

Above: Landing on water is difficult for large birds, such as pelicans (Pelecanidae), which slow their descent by gliding on open wings.

Wing shape and beat

The shape of the wing is important for a bird's flying ability. Birds that remain airborne for much of their lives, such as albatrosses, have relatively long wings that allow them to glide with relatively little effort. The wandering albatross (*Diomedea exulans*) has the largest wingspan of any bird, measuring about 3.4m (11ft) from one wing tip to the other. Large, heavy birds such as the Himalayan vulture (*Gyps himalayensis*) often experience difficulty in flying early in the day, before the land has warmed up. This is because there is insufficient heat coming up from the ground to create the thermal air currents that help to keep them airborne. In common with other large birds of prey, Himalayan vultures seek out these rising columns of air, which provide uplift, and then circle around in them.

The number of wing beats varies dramatically between different species. Sunbirds (Nectariniidae) prove very agile in flight, although they are not able to hover in front of flowers like the hummingbirds of America, whose wings move so fast – at 200 beats per minute or more – that they appear as a blur to our eyes. At the other extreme, heavy birds such as swans fly with slow, deliberate wing beats.

Lightening the load

It is not just the lightness of the bird's skeleton that helps it to fly. There have been evolutionary changes in the body organs too, most noticeably in the urinary system. Unlike mammals, birds do not have a bladder that fills with urine. Instead, their urine is greatly concentrated, in the form of uric acid, and passes out of the body with their faeces, appearing as a creamy-white, semi-solid component.

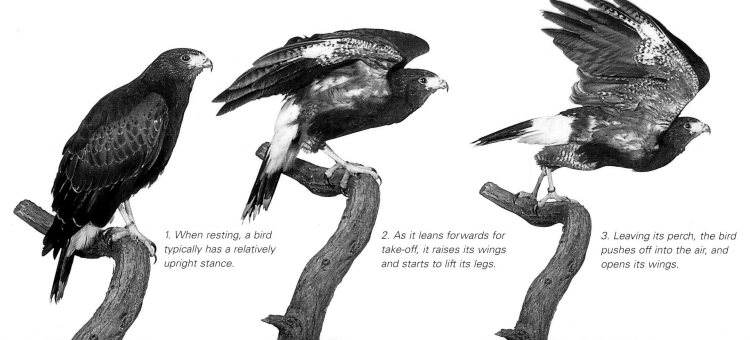

1. When resting, a bird typically has a relatively upright stance.

2. As it leans forwards for take-off, it raises its wings and starts to lift its legs.

3. Leaving its perch, the bird pushes off into the air, and opens its wings.

Above: Owls such as this bobook owl (Ninox novaeseelandiae) have acquired a reputation as silent hunters of the night. Their expansive wings lessen the need for noisy flapping.

Below: The black-browed albatross (Diomedea melanophris) and its relatives often skim just above the waves.

The aerofoil principle

Once in flight, the shape of the wing is crucial in keeping the bird airborne. Viewed in cross-section from the side, a bird's wing resembles an aircraft's wing, called an aerofoil, since aircraft also use this principle to fly.

The wing is curved across the top, so the movement of air is faster over this part of the wing compared with the lower surface. This produces reduced air pressure on top of the wing, which provides lift and makes it easier for the bird to stay in the air.

The long flight feathers at the rear edge of the wings help to provide the thrust and lift for flight. The tail feathers, too, can help the bird remain airborne. The Australian kestrel (*Falco cenchroides*), for example, having spotted prey on the ground, spreads its tail feathers to help it remain aloft while it hovers to target its prey.

A bird's wings move in a regular figure-of-eight movement while it is in flight. During the downstroke, the flight feathers join together to push powerfully against the air. The primary flight feathers bend backwards, which propels the bird forwards. As the wing moves upwards, the longer primary flight feathers move apart, which reduces air resistance. The secondary feathers further along the wing provide some slight propulsion. After that the cycle repeats itself.

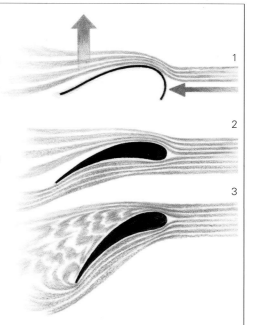

Above: The flow of air over a bird's wing varies according to the wing's position.
1. When the wing is stretched out horizontally, an area of low pressure is created above the wing, causing lift.
2. As the wing is tilted downwards, the flow of the air is disrupted, causing turbulence and loss of lift.
3. When the wing is angled downwards, lift slows, which results in stalling, with the wing acting as a brake.

Flight patterns and formations

Different species of birds have various ways of flying, which can actually aid the birdwatcher in helping to identify them. For example, small birds such as tits (Paridae) and finches (Fringillidae) alternately flap their wings and fold them at their sides, adopting a streamlined shape, which helps to save energy. This produces a characteristic dipping flight. Large birds such as ducks and geese maintain a straighter course at an even height.

In some cases, it is not just the individual flying skills of a bird that can help it to stay airborne, but those of its fellows nearby. Birds flying in formation create a slipstream, which makes flying less effort for all the birds behind the leader. This is why birds often fly in formation, especially when covering large distances on migration.

4. Powerful upward and downward sweeps of the wings propel the bird forwards.

5. When coming in to land, a bird lowers its legs and slows its wing movements.

6. Braking is achieved by a vertical landing posture, with the tail feathers spread.

LOCOMOTION

For most birds, flight is the main means of locomotion. However, the ability to move on the ground or in water can be vital, particularly when it comes to obtaining food. Some birds have even lost the ability to fly, relying instead on their swimming or running skills to escape predators and find food.

Not all birds possess the ability to fly, but this does not mean they are handicapped in their natural environment. Penguins may appear to be rather clumsy shuffling around on land, but they are extremely well adapted to life in the water. Like other primarily aquatic birds, their webbed feet enable them to swim very effectively. Webbing is a common feature seen in aquatic birds. The skin folds linking the toes turn the foot into an effective paddle, allowing the bird to maximize its propulsive forward thrust by pushing against the water. On land, however, webbed feet do impose certain restrictions, because being linked together in this way means that the individual toes are not as flexible.

Aquatic locomotion

When penguins dive, their sleek, torpedo-shaped bodies allow them to swim fast underwater, reaching speeds equivalent to 40km/h (25mph). Their flippers, which evolved from wings,

Below: A group of king penguins (Aptenodytes patagonicus) leap in and out of the water as they swim along, in a form of movement known as porpoising.

help them to steer very effectively as they pursue fish, which form the basis of their diet. Like flying birds, penguins need effective wing muscles to control their movements, so their skeletal structure bears a close similarity to that of flying birds.

Flightless ducks and other aquatic birds, such as the Galapagos Island cormorant (*Nannopterum harrisi*), use a different method of locomotion: they rely entirely on their feet rather than their wings for propulsive power. Their skeletons differ from those of flying birds in that they lack the prominent keel on the sternum for the attachment of flight muscles.

Flightless land birds

A number of land birds have lost the ability to fly. Typically, they are birds that inhabit islands where, until the arrival of cats and rats brought by ships from Europe, they faced few if any predators. The arrival of predators has left them vulnerable, and many have since become extinct, including the dodo (*Raphus cucullatus*), a large, flightless pigeon from the island of Mauritius in the Indian Ocean. A high percentage of flightless birds evolved

Above: Penguins such as the chinstrap (Pygoscelis antarctica) are less agile on land than they are in the sea, where their body shape lessens water resistance.

on the islands of New Zealand, but many have since vanished, including all species of moa (*Dinornis* and related forms). Moas represent the most diverse group of flightless birds ever recorded. The last examples probably died out about the time of European settlement of these islands in the 19th century.

The giant moa (*Dinornis maximus*) was the largest member of the group and, indeed, the tallest bird ever to have existed. It would have dwarfed today's ostriches, standing up to 3.5m (11.5ft) high. There may have been as many as a dozen or more different types of moa, which filled the same sort of niche as grazing mammals, which were absent from New Zealand.

In the absence of predatory mammals, the moas faced no significant threats to their survival until the first human settlers reached New Zealand and started to hunt them. Their large size made them conspicuous, and, having evolved in an environment where they had been safe from persecution, they had lost their ability to fly. Moas were not even able to run fast, in contrast to modern flightless birds such as ostriches. These defenceless giants were soon driven to extinction.

Circulation

The circulatory system is vital in supporting the activities of both flighted and flightless birds, ensuring that their muscles are well supplied with oxygen. The heart acts as the pump, driving the blood around the body. The basic design of the heart is similar to that of a mammal, with the left side being highly developed because it does more work. Overall, the heart rate of birds is much more rapid than mammals of similar size, having been measured at 1,000 beats per minute in the case of canaries at rest. The heart beat rises dramatically during flight, but soon returns to normal when the bird touches down.

The respiratory system

Birds have lungs, located close to the vertebral column, but these do not expand and contract in the same way as those of mammals. Instead, birds rely on a series of air sacs that act rather like bellows, to suck

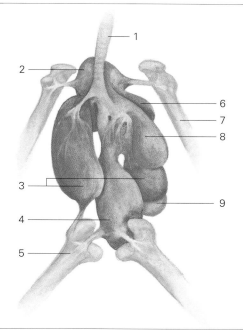

air through their respiratory system. In some cases, these link with the hollow limb bones, and thus help to meet the bird's high requirement for oxygen when flying. A bird's respiratory rate is a reflection of its body size, as well as its level of activity and lifestyle. Common starlings (*Sturnus vulgaris*), for example, typically breathe about 85 times every minute, whereas domestic chickens, which are more sedentary, have an equivalent respiratory rate of only about 20 breaths per minute.

1 Trachea
2 Interclavicular air sac
3 Lungs
4 Abdominal air sac
5 Femur (leg bone)
6 Cervical air sac
7 Humerus (wing bone)
8 Anterior thoracic air sac
9 Posterior thoracic air sac

Above: The razor-sharp inner claw of the cassowary (Casuarius unappendiculatus) *is able to disembowel a person, making these birds very dangerous.*

Ratites

Not all flightless birds are helpless in the face of danger, however. The large, flightless birds known as ratites, including cassowaries, ostriches, emus and rheas, are particularly well able to defend themselves. Their strong legs are quite capable of inflicting lethal blows, especially in the case of the cassowaries (Casuariidae), found in parts of northern Australia, New Guinea and neighbouring islands. These birds have an elongated and deadly sharp claw on their innermost toe. If the cassowary is cornered and unable to run away, it lashes out with its legs and is quite capable of disembowelling a person with its

claws. The bird also has a hard, bony crest called a casque, which protects the top of its head.

Although there are only three species of cassowary, confined to New Guinea and adjacent islands as well as Australia, they are split into as many as 21 different subspecies, which vary in minor respects. This is a reflection of the way in which the individual populations have developed in relative isolation from each other, often inhabiting islands divided by large stretches of water, and is a common phenomenon in birds found in this part of the world.

The large ratites all share a similar shape, having bulky bodies, long legs, no more than three toes per foot (most birds possess four), and long, slender necks. Like all flightless birds, they do possess wings, which help them to maintain their balance and may also be used as part of an elaborate display. Emus (*Dromaius novaehollandiae*), however, do not even use their strictly rudimentary wings to draw attention to themselves.

Kiwis (Apterygidae) are also ratites, but they are much smaller birds with shorter legs. Unlike other ratites, they are not fast runners, but rely on camouflage and their nocturnal habits to conceal their presence from predators, rather than speed to escape.

Running in flighted birds

Some birds that are able to fly still prefer to use their running abilities to obtain food and escape danger. They include the blue-crowned pigeons (*Goura cristata*) of New Guinea. With their short wings, these birds can fly clumsily, but prefer to use their strong legs to overtake and pounce on prey. In general, flying uses a lot of energy compared to running or hopping. Many birds choose to move swiftly over the ground to seize prey or avoid an enemy if they judge that the situation does not warrant flight.

Below: The height and keen eyesight of emus (Dromaius novaehollandiae) *makes them hard to ambush in open country. Their pace allows them to escape from danger with little difficulty, while their long stride length when running enables them to cover large amounts of ground in a single step.*

AVIAN SENSES

The keen senses of birds are vital to their survival, in particular helping them to find food, escape from enemies and find mates in the breeding season. Sight is the primary sense for most birds, but some species rely heavily on other senses to thrive in particular habitats.

All birds' senses are well adapted to their environment, and the shape of the body can help to reflect which senses are most significant to them.

Sight and lifestyle

Most birds rely on their sense of sight to avoid danger, hunt for food and locate familiar surroundings. The importance of this sense is reflected by the size of their eyes, with those of

Field of vision

The positioning of a bird's eyes on its head affects its field of vision. The eyes of owls are positioned to face forwards, producing an overlapping image of the area in front known as binocular vision. This allows the owl to pinpoint its prey exactly, so that it can strike. In contrast, the eyes of birds that are likely to be preyed upon, such as woodcocks, are positioned on the sides of the head. This eye position gives a greatly reduced area of binocular vision, but it does give these birds practically all-round vision, enabling them to spot danger from all sides.

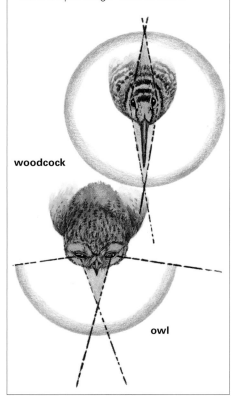

woodcock

owl

starlings (*Sturnus vulgaris*), for example, making up 15 per cent of the total head weight. The enlargement of the eyeballs and associated structures, notably the eye sockets in the skull, has altered the shape of the brain. In addition, the optic lobes in the brain, which are concerned with vision, are also enlarged, whereas the olfactory counterparts, responsible for smell, are poorly developed.

The structure of the eye also reveals much about a bird's habits. Birds of prey have large eyes in proportion to their head, and have correspondingly keen eyesight. Species that regularly hunt for prey underwater, such as penguins, can see well in the water. They have a muscle in each eye that reduces the diameter of the lens and increases its thickness on entering water, so that their eyes can adjust easily to seeing underwater. In addition, certain diving birds such as penguins (Spheniscidae) use a lens that forms part of the nictitating membrane, or third eyelid, which is normally hidden from sight. Underwater, when this membrane covers the eye, its convex shape serves as a lens, helping the bird to see in these surroundings.

Eye position

The positioning of the eyes on the head gives important clues to a bird's lifestyle. Most birds' eyes are set on the sides of the head. Owls, however, have flattened faces and forward-facing eyes that are critical to their hunting ability. These features allow owls to target their prey.

There are disadvantages, though – owls' eyes do not give a rounded view of the world, so they must turn their heads to see around them. It is not just the positioning of owls' eyes that is unusual. They are also able to hunt effectively in almost complete darkness. This is made possible in two

Above: Kiwis (Apteryx australis) *have smaller eyes than most birds, and therefore rely more heavily on their sense of smell when foraging for food.*

ways. First, their pupils are large, which maximizes the amount of light passing through to the retina behind the lens, where the image is formed. Second, the cells here consist mainly of rods rather than cones. While cones give good colour vision, rods function to create images when background illumination is low.

The positioning of the eyes of game birds such as woodcocks (*Scolopax rusticola*) allows them to spot danger from almost any angle. It is even possible for them to see a predator sneaking up from behind. Their only blind spot is just behind the head.

Smell

Very few birds have a sense of smell, but kiwis (Apterygidae) and vultures (forming part of the order Falciformes) are notable exceptions. Birds' nostrils are normally located above the bill, opening directly into the skull, but kiwis' nostrils are positioned right at the end of the long bill. They probably help these birds to locate earthworms

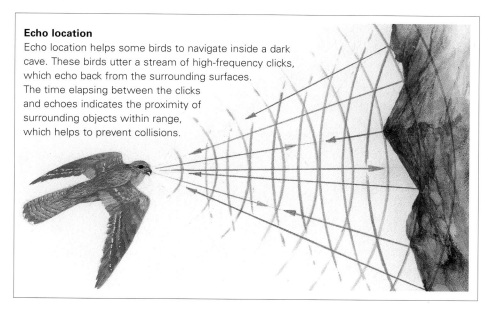

Echo location
Echo location helps some birds to navigate inside a dark cave. These birds utter a stream of high-frequency clicks, which echo back from the surrounding surfaces. The time elapsing between the clicks and echoes indicates the proximity of surrounding objects within range, which helps to prevent collisions.

in the soil. Vultures have very keen eyesight, which helps them to spot dead animals on the ground from the air, but they also have a strong sense of smell, which helps when homing in on a distant carcass.

Taste

The senses of smell and taste are linked, and most birds also have correspondingly few taste buds in their mouths. The number of taste buds varies, with significant differences between groups of birds. Pigeons may have as few as 50 taste buds in their mouths, parrots as many as 400.

Birds' taste buds are located all around the mouth, rather than just on the tongue, as in mammals. The close

Below: The eyes of diving birds such as the emperor penguin (Aptenodytes forsteri) are covered by a transparent membrane when they are underwater. Penguins swallow their prey whole, so taste is of little significance.

links between smell and taste can lead vultures, which feed only on fresh carcasses, to reject decomposing meat. They may start to eat it, but then spit it out once it is in their mouths, probably because of a combination of bad odour and taste.

Hearing

Birds generally do not have a highly developed sense of hearing. They lack any external ear flaps that would help to pinpoint sources of sound. The openings to their hearing system are located on the sides of the head, back from the eyes.

Hearing is of particular significance for nocturnal species, such as owls, which find their food in darkness. These birds are highly attuned to the calls made by rodents. The broad shape of their skull has the additional advantage of spacing the ear openings more widely, which helps them to localize the source of the sounds with greater accuracy.

Hearing is also important to birds during the breeding season. Birds show particular sensitivity to sounds falling within the vocal range of their chicks, which helps them to locate their offspring easily in the critical early days after fledging.

Various cave swiftlets (*Aerodramus*), which are found in many parts of eastern Asia, use echo location to find their way around in the dark, rather like bats. Unlike the sounds bats make,

however, the clicking sounds of the swiftlet's calls – up to 20 a second in darkness – are clearly audible to humans. The bird interprets the echoes of its call to avoid colliding with objects in its path, although it also uses its eyesight when flying. The oilbird (*Steatornis caripensis*) from South America, which also dwells in dark caves, uses a similar method.

Touch

The sense of touch is more developed in some birds than others. Those such as snipe (*Gallinago*), which have long bills for seeking food, have sensitive nerve endings called corpuscles in their bills that pick up tiny vibrations caused by their prey. Vibrations that could suggest approaching danger can also register via other corpuscles located particularly in the legs, so that the bird has a sensory awareness even when it is resting on a branch.

Wind-borne sensing

Tubenoses such as albatrosses and petrels (Procellariiformes) have a valve in each nostril that fills with air as the bird flies. These are affected by both the bird's speed and the wind strength. The valves almost certainly act as a type of wind gauge, allowing these birds to detect changes in wind strength and patterns. This information helps to keep them airborne, as they skim over the waves with minimal effort.

Below: A combination of senses, especially eyesight, helps cattle egrets (Bubulcus ibis) to detect food, whether they are merely poised to hunt or actually scavenging. These are highly adaptable birds by nature.

PLANT-EATERS

All over the world, many birds depend on plant matter as part of their diet, with seeds and nuts in particular providing nourishment. A close relationship between plants and birds exists in many cases. Birds fertilize flowers when feeding on nectar, and help to spread their seeds when eating fruit.

Many different types of birds are primarily plant-eaters, whether feeding on flowers, fruit, nuts and seeds, or other plant matter. Plant-eating species have to eat a large volume of food compared to meat-eating species, because of the low nutritional value of plants compared with that of prey such as invertebrates.

In the last century or so, many species have benefited from the spread of agriculture, which now provides them with large acreages of suitable crop plants to feed on. These birds' feeding habits bring them into conflict with farmers when they breed rapidly in response to a swift expansion in their food supply. For example, populations of bare-eyed corellas (*Cacatua sanguinea*) have increased quickly in Australia thanks to the spread of arable agriculture there, and

Below: The pied imperial pigeon (Ducula bicolor) is predominantly white in colour, although its head is often stained yellow with the juice of fruits and berries. The fondness of these birds for wild figs and nutmeg has earned them the alias "nutmeg pigeons".

the associated provision of reservoirs for irrigation purposes. These birds have bred up to form huge flocks comprising many thousands of individuals, which inflict massive damage on crops as they ripen. They are now labelled as pests in some areas.

Adapting to changing seasons

Birds from temperate areas exist on a varied diet that is related to the seasons. Bullfinches (*Pyrrhula pyrrhula*), for example, eat the buds in apple orchards in spring – when they can become a pest – while later in the year, they consume seeds and fruit. Their bills, like those of most other members of the finch family, are stout and relatively conical, which helps them to crack seeds effectively.

Some birds store plant food when it is plentiful, to sustain them through the winter. Nutcrackers (*Nucifraga*) collect hazel nuts, which they feed on in winter until the following year. Acorn woodpeckers (*Melanerpes formicivorus*), of America, drill holes in trees and fill them with acorns, creating an accessible larder for the winter, when snow covers the ground.

Flowers

A number of birds rely on flowers rather than the whole plant as a source of food. Pollen is a valuable source of protein, while nectar provides sugars. Not surprisingly, flower-feeders tend to be confined to mainly tropical areas, where flowers are in bloom throughout the year. Sunbirds (Nectariniidae), for instance, use their narrow bills to probe into flowers to obtain nectar. Some sunbirds have developed especially curved or elongated bills, which allow them to feed on particular flowers. These birds help to pollinate the plants on which they feed by transferring pollen from flower to flower on their bills or even on plumage.

The digestive system

Birds lack teeth, so their food must be swallowed whole. Birds have a storage organ known as the crop, which is located at the base of the neck. From here, food passes down into the proventriculus, where the digestive process starts, before entering the gizzard, which is equivalent to the mammalian stomach. Nutrients are then absorbed through the wall of the small intestine.

The digestive system of plant-eaters differs in various respects from that of predatory species. Vegetable matter is less nourishing than meat, so plant-eaters generally need longer digestive tracts to process the large quantities of food they must consume in order to obtain enough nourishment. In addition, digesting plant matter poses certain difficulties. The gizzards of seed-eating species such as many finches (Fringillidae) have especially thick muscular walls, which serve to grind up the seeds.

1 Oesophagus	6 Large intestine
2 Crop	7 Liver
3 Proventriculus	8 Spleen
4 Pancreas	9 Small intestine
5 Gizzard	

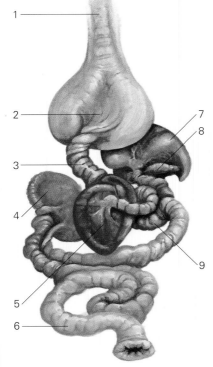

Plant matter

Relatively few birds feed almost entirely on herbage, although there are some exceptions. The primitive hoatzin (*Opisthocomus hoazin*), from South America, has a highly specialized diet consisting mainly of marsh plants, which restricts it to the mangrove forests of the Amazon basin. Turacos (Musophagidae) of Africa feed mainly on leaves, while parrots such as the eclectus (*Eclectus roratus*) seem to prefer plant matter to fruit or seeds.

The breakdown of vegetation presents considerable difficulty, since birds do not possess the necessary enzymes to digest the cellulose in plants. Birds such as grouse (Tetraoninae), which feed regularly on plant matter, have evolved long, blind-ending tubes known as caeca. These contain beneficial microbes that can break down cellulose.

Nuts and seeds

These dry foods are a valuable resource to many different types of birds, ranging from parrots to finches. However, cracking the tough outer shell or husk can be a problem. Finches such as grosbeaks have evolved a particularly strong bill for this purpose. Hawfinches (*Coccothraustes coccothraustes*) are able to crack cherry stones (pits) to extract the kernel.

Above: The bill of this fork-tailed sunbird (Aethopyga christinae) *is typically long and narrow. The tongue runs almost the entire length of the bill and enables the bird to feed on nectar by means of powerful suction.*

Sunbirds (Nectariniidae) are found mainly in Africa and Asia, with a single species extending to Australia. They fill a similar evolutionary role to hummingbirds, which they resemble in their small size and bright, colourful and often iridescent plumage. Unlike hummingbirds, however, they are not able to feed during flight, but have to perch within reach of the flower to suck up the nectar. Various members of the parrot family also feed on flowers, notably lories and lorikeets. Their tongues are equipped with tiny, bristle-like projections called papillae, which enable them to collect pollen easily.

Fruit

Exclusively frugivorous (fruit-eating) birds such as fruit doves (*Ptilinopus*) are found only in the tropics, where fruit is available throughout the year. These species usually dwell in tropical rainforests, where they help to protect the biodiversity of the forest by passing seeds of the fruits they eat directly through their digestive tract, to be deposited far from the parent plant, which helps the plants to spread.

Above: A flock of wild rainbow lorikeets (Trichoglossus haematodus) *in Queensland, Australia. These colourful birds feed on nectar and fruit. In some areas, they are so tame that they will descend to feed on honey and cake put out for them in suburban gardens.*

The most bizarre example of bill adaptation for eating seeds is seen in the crossbills (*Loxia*) of northern coniferous forests. These birds have literally twisted upper and lower mandibles, which help them to crack open the seeds inside the larch cones, which they eat. Some cockatoos such as the Moluccan (*Cacatua moluccensis*) have bills that are even strong enough to open coconuts.

Below: Black swans (Cygnus atratus) *are just as adept at using their long neck and large bill for grazing on the land as when obtaining food from below the water's surface.*

PREDATORS AND SCAVENGERS

Just as with other vertebrates, there is a food chain within the avian kingdom. Some species hunt only other birds, while others seek a more varied range of prey, including, commonly, invertebrates. Even birds that feed mainly on seeds catch protein-rich insects to feed their chicks in the nest.

Some birds are active predators, seeking and killing their own food, while others prefer to scavenge on carcasses. Many predatory birds are opportunistic, hunting when food is plentiful but scavenging when it becomes scarce. Both hunters and scavengers have evolved to live in a wide range of environments, and display correspondingly diverse hunting skills to obtain their food.

Birds of prey have sharp bills that enable them to tear the flesh of their prey into strips small enough to swallow. Eating whole animals can potentially cause digestive problems for these birds because of the bones, skin, feathers and other relatively indigestible body parts. Owls overcome this problem by regurgitating pellets composed of the indigestible remains of their prey. Kingfishers produce similar pellets of fish bones and scales. These are of value to zoologists studying the feeding habits of such birds.

Below: Peregrine falcons (Falco peregrinus) *are adept aerial hunters, with pigeons – including homing pigeons – featuring prominently in their diet. These birds of prey display not just speed, but also superb manoeuvrability in flight, when pursuing their quarry.*

Birds of prey
Some avian predators feed mainly on other birds, such as the grey goshawk (*Accipiter novaehollandiae*). Some females are large enough to overpower herons, although pigeons, slow and clumsy in flight, make easier targets. Another bird-eater, the peregrine falcon (*Falco peregrinus*), is among the most agile of all hunting birds. Strength is a feature of some species that prey on mammals, such as the golden eagle (*Aquila chrysaetos*), which can lift a young lamb in its powerful talons, but often opts to feed on carrion. Other species target fish

Above: Vision is the main sense that allows most birds of prey, such as golden eagles (Aquila chrysaetos), *to target their victims. These eagles have keen sight.*

and reptiles; the large number of birds that eat invertebrates such as insects are not usually known as birds of prey.

Hunting techniques
Many predatory birds hunt during the day, but not all, with most owls preferring to seek their prey at night. Mice and other creatures that are caught by owls are killed and eaten immediately. In contrast, shrikes (Laniidae) have a grisly reputation because they kill more prey than they can eat immediately. They store the surplus as a so-called larder. They impale invertebrates such as grasshoppers, and even sometimes small vertebrates, on to sharp vegetation, and return to feed on them later. Caching, as this behaviour is known, is especially common during the breeding period, and presumably developed as a way of ensuring that the shrikes have sufficient food to rear their young.

Some birds have evolved particular ways of overcoming prey in certain localities. In parts of Egypt, for example, eagles have learnt to prey on

Above: Like other cormorants, the white-necked cormorant (Phalacrocorax carbo) brings fish that it catches underwater up to the surface before swallowing them.

tortoises by seizing the unfortunate reptiles in their talons, and then dropping them on to rocky ground from the air to split open their shells.

Not all birds of prey are aerial predators. Species such as secretary birds (*Sagittarius serpentarius*), which range widely across Africa in grassland areas, prefer to seek their victims on the ground. Secretary birds have developed long, strong legs and yet have surprisingly small feet. Snakes feature prominently in the diet of these birds, which raise their wings when confronting one of the reptiles. This has the effect of breaking up the bird's outline, making it harder for the snake to strike. Meanwhile the bird uses its feet to stun the reptile by jumping up and down on it, before killing it with a stab of its sharp bill.

Aquatic predators

The osprey (*Pandion haliaetus*) is an unusual bird of prey that literally scoops up large fish swimming close to the water's surface while in flight. Other birds actually enter the water in search of their prey. They may not have sharp talons, but many have powerful bills that enable them to grab slippery fish without difficulty.

Pelicans are equipped with a large, capacious pouch beneath the lower part of their bill, which they use like a net to trawl the water for fish.

Cormorants (Phalacrocoracidae) dive down after fish, and can remain submerged for some time. Kingfishers (*Alcedo atthis*) have sharp eyesight. Having detected the presence of a fish from the air, they dive into the water, seizing their quarry in their pointed bill and then re-emerging immediately. They then kill the fish by battering it against their perch. The speed at which the kingfisher dives provides the momentum it needs to break through the surface, and it closes its wings once submerged to reduce resistance.

Aquatic predators always try to swallow fish head-first. That way, gills and scales do not get stuck in their throat. On land, predatory birds that hunt victims such as rodents employ a similar technique so they do not choke on fur and tails.

Scavengers

Vultures are the best-known of all scavengers. They can home in on carcasses from a great distance away, and so have become regarded as harbingers of death. Lammergeiers (*Gypaetus barbatus*) have developed a technique that allows them to feed on bones that their relatives cannot break open. They smash the bones into pieces by dropping them from a great height. It is a skill that they learn to perfect by choosing the right terrain on which to drop the bones.

Despite their grim reputation, vultures serve an important purpose in many densely populated Asian cities,

Above: Precise judgement from a perch allows a kingfisher (Alcedo atthis) to strike with deadly accuracy into clear water.

where they feed almost entirely on the carcasses of cattle. India's vulture population has fallen by an alarming rate in recent years, with one region reporting a ninety per cent drop in the number of white-backed vultures (*Gyps bengalensis*) over less than a decade. Various factors are being blamed for the decline, including pest control (such as poisoning and shooting), insecticides, and even a virus that seems to cause renal and visceral gout in the birds. But the lack of competition from these scavengers has prompted a growing number of feral dogs, many of which have rabies, to roam the streets in search of scraps.

Below: The bald head of the griffon vulture (Gyps fulvus) is useful when feeding, as any plumage would become matted with blood.

DISPLAY AND PAIRING

Birds' breeding habits vary greatly. Some birds pair up only fleetingly, while others do so for the whole breeding season, and some species pair for life. For many young cock birds, the priority is to gain a territory as the first step in attracting a partner. Birds use both plumage and their songs to attract a mate.

A number of factors trigger the onset of the breeding period. In temperate areas, as the days start to lengthen in spring, the increase in daylight is detected by the pineal gland in the bird's brain, which starts a complex series of hormonal changes in the body. Most birds form a bond with a single partner during the breeding season, which is often preceded by an elaborate display by the cock bird.

Bird song

Many cock birds announce their presence by their song, which both attracts would-be mates and establishes a claim to a territory. Once pairing has occurred, the male may cease singing, but in some cases he starts to perform a duet with the hen, with each bird singing in turn.

Singing obviously serves to keep members of the pair in touch with each other. In species such as Central and

Below: A cock Wilson's bird of paradise (Cicinnurus respublica) displaying. Bright plumage is often a feature of members of this family, but cock birds gain their breeding finery only slowly by progressive moults over several years. They move up through the display hierarchy until they can obtain a mate.

Above: A male ruff (Philomachus pugnax) at a lek, where males compete with each other in displays to attract female partners. Ruffs do not form lasting pair bonds, so the hens nest on their own after mating has occurred.

South American wood quails (*Odontophorus*), the pair co-ordinate their songs so precisely that although the cock bird may sing the first few notes, and then the hen, it sounds as if the song is being sung by just one bird. Other birds may sing in unison. With African gonoleks (*Laniarius*), it may even be possible to tell the length of time that the pair have been together by the degree of harmony in their particular songs.

Studies have revealed that young male birds start warbling quite quietly, and then sing more loudly as they mature. Finally, when their song pattern becomes fixed, it remains constant throughout the bird's life.

It is obviously possible to identify different species by differences in their song patterns. However, there are sometimes marked variations between the songs of individuals of the same species that live in different places. Local dialects have been identified in various parts of a species' distribution, as in the case of mynahs (Sturnidae) from various parts of New Guinea. In addition, as far as some songbirds are concerned, recent studies have shown

Below: A pair of musk lorikeets (Glossopsitta concinna), which are found in eastern parts of Australia and on Tasmania. Mutual preening is a familiar sight among these birds during the breeding season, as it serves to strengthen the bond between parents, and therefore enhance the survival of the family unit. Some parrots may pair for life with a single partner.

Above: Mute swans (Cygnus olor) *are one of the species that pair for life. They become highly territorial when breeding, but outside the nesting period they often form flocks on large stretches of water. In spite of their common name, they can vocalize to a limited extent, by hissing and even grunting.*

that over the course of several generations, the pattern of song can alter markedly.

Birds produce their sounds – even those species capable of mimicking human speech – without the benefit of a larynx and vocal cords like humans. The song is created in a voice organ called the syrinx, which is located in the bird's throat, at the bottom of the windpipe, or trachea.

The structure of the syrinx is very variable, being at its most highly developed in the case of songbirds, which possess as many as nine pairs of separate muscles to control the vocal output. As in the human larynx, it is the movement of air through the syrinx that enables the membranes here to vibrate, creating sound. An organ called the interclavicular air sac also plays an important role in sound production, and birds cannot sing without it. The distance over which bird calls can travel is remarkable – up to 5km (3 miles) in the case of some species, such as various bitterns (*Botaurus*), which are renowned for their particularly deep and penetrating song, amplified by the gullet.

Breeding behaviour

Many birds rely on their breeding finery to attract their mates. Some groups assemble in communal display areas known as leks, where hens witness the males' displays and select a mate. A number of different species, ranging from various members of the grouse family (Tetraoninae) to birds of paradise (Paradisaeidae), establish leks.

In other species, such as the satin bowerbird (*Ptilonorhynchus violaceus*), the male constructs elaborate bowers of grass, twigs and similar vegetation that he decorates with items of a particular colour, such as blue, varying from flowers to pieces of glass. Male bowerbirds are often polygamous,

meaning that they mate with more than one female. Weaver birds, such as the baya weaver (*Ploceus philippinus*), demonstrate the same behaviour. The males moult to display brightly coloured plumage at the onset of the breeding season, and construct nests that are inspected by the females. Hens are often drawn to the older cocks, whose nest-building abilities are likely to be more sophisticated.

Pair bonding

Many birds form no lasting male-female partnership, although the pair bond may be strong during the nesting period. It is usually only in potentially long-lived species, such as the larger parrots and macaws, or in relatively long-lived waterfowl such as swans, that a life-long pair bond is formed.

Pair bonding in long-lived species has certain advantages. The young of such birds are slow to mature, and are often unlikely to nest for five years or more. By remaining for a time in a protective and nurturing family unit, the adults can improve the long-term survival prospects of their young.

Below: The dance of Japanese cranes (Grus japonensis) *is one of the most spectacular sights in the avian world, reinforcing the life-long pair bond in this species. Dancing starts with the trumpeting calls of the birds as they stand side-by-side. Both sexes then start to leap into the air and display, raising their wings and tail feathers. Sometimes the birds even pick up sticks and toss them into the air.*

NESTING AND EGG-LAYING

All birds reproduce by laying eggs, which are covered with a hard, calcareous shell. The number of eggs laid at a time – known as the clutch size – varies significantly between species, as does egg coloration. Nesting habits also vary, with some birds constructing very elaborate nests.

The coloration and markings of a bird's eggs are directly linked to the nesting site. Birds that usually breed in hollow trees produce white eggs, because these are normally hidden from predators and so do not need to be camouflaged. The pale coloration may also help the adult birds to locate the eggs as they return to the nest, thus lessening the chances of damaging them. Birds that build open, cup-shaped nests tend to lay coloured and often mottled eggs that are camouflaged and so less obvious to potential nest thieves.

Nesting holes

Many birds use tree holes for nesting. Woodpeckers (Picidae) are particularly well equipped to create nesting chambers, using their powerful bills to enlarge holes in dead trees. The diameter of the entry hole thus created

Below: The eggs of emus (Dromaius novaehollandiae) rank amongst the largest laid by any bird in Asia or Australia. They range in weight from 450–800g (18–32oz), and take around 8 weeks to hatch. Beneath the dark green exterior lie two further layers of colour: a layer of teal, and a thinner coating of white.

Above: A pair of crimson-breasted wood-peckers (Dendrocopus cathpharius). Tree holes offer relatively safe nesting retreats, although snakes may be able to reach them. These birds can excavate their own nest sites.

is just wide enough to allow the birds to enter easily, which helps to prevent the nest being robbed. Hornbills (Bucorvidae) go one stage further – the cock bird walls the hen up inside the nest. He plasters the hole over with mud, leaving just a small gap through which he can feed the female. The barrier helps to protect the nest from attacks by snakes and lizards. The female remains entombed inside until her young are well grown. At this stage she breaks out and then helps her mate to rear the chicks, having walled them back up again.

Nest-building

Some birds return to the same nest site each year, but many birds simply abandon their old nest and build another. This may seem a waste of effort, but it actually helps to protect the birds from parasites such as blood-sucking mites, which can otherwise multiply in the confines of the nest. Most birds construct their nests from vegetation, depending on which

The reproductive systems

The cock bird has two testes located within his body. Spermatozoa pass down the vas deferens, into the cloaca and then out of the body. Insemination occurs when the vent areas of the male and female bird are in direct contact during mating. Cock birds do not have a penis for penetration, although certain groups, such as waterfowl, may have a primitive organ that is used to assist in the transference of semen in a similar way.

Normally only the left ovary and oviduct of the hen bird are functional. Eggs pass down through the reproductive tract from the ovary. Spermatozoa swim up the hen's reproductive tract, and fertilize the ova at an early stage in the process. Generally, only one mating is required to fertilize a clutch of eggs. Spermatozoa may sometimes remain viable in the hen's body for up to three weeks following mating.

1 Kidneys	7 Magnum
2 Testes	8 Isthmus
3 Vas deferens	9 Egg with shell
4 Cloaca	contained in
	the hen's
5 Ova	reproductive tract
6 Infundibulum	10 Cloaca

Male   **Female**

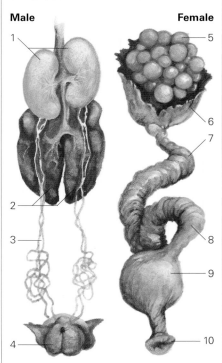

materials are locally available. In coastal areas, some seabirds use pieces of seaweed to build theirs. Artificial materials such as plastic wrappers or polystyrene may be used by some birds.

Nest styles

Different types of birds build nests of various shapes and sizes, which are characteristic of their species. Groups such as finches build nests in the form of an open cup, often concealed in vegetation. Most pigeons and doves construct a loose platform of twigs. Swallows are among the birds that use mud to construct their nests. They scoop muddy water up from the surface of a pond or puddle, mould it into shape on a suitable wall, and then allow it to dry and harden like cement.

The simplest nests are composed of little more than a pad of material, resting in the fork of a tree or on a building. The effort entailed in nest construction may reflect how often the birds are likely to nest. The platforms of pigeons and doves can disintegrate quite easily, resulting in the loss of eggs or chicks. However, if disaster does befall the nest, the pair will often breed again within a few weeks. At the other end of the scale, albatrosses expend considerable effort on nesting, because if failure occurs, the pair may not breed again for two years or so.

Cup-shaped nests are more elaborate than platform nests, being usually made by weaving grasses and twigs together. The inside is often lined with soft feathers. The raised sides of the cup nest lessen the likelihood of losing eggs and chicks, and also offer greater security to the adults during incubation. The hollow in the nest's centre is created by the birds compressing the material here before egg-laying begins.

Suspended nests enclosed by a domed roof offer even greater security. They are less accessible to predators because of their design and also their position, often hanging from slender branches. Some waxbills (Estrildidae) build a particularly elaborate nest, comprising two chambers. There is an obvious upper opening, which is

Above: Tropic birds favour secluded islands for breeding. They will often choose a site such as this, among boulders or beneath a rocky outcrop, for concealment.

always empty, suggesting to would-be predators that the nest is unoccupied. The birds occupy the chamber beneath, which has a separate opening.

Nest protection

Some birds rely on the safety of numbers to deter would-be predators, building vast communal nests that are occupied by successive generations and added to regularly. Monk parakeets (*Myiopsitta monarchus*), from South America, breed in this way. Their nests may weigh over 200kg (4cwt).

Other birds have evolved more sophisticated methods of not only protecting their nests, but also of minimizing the time that they spend

incubating their eggs. Various parrots, such as the golden-shouldered parakeet (*Psephotus chrysopterygius*), from Australia, lay their eggs in termite mounds. The insects tolerate this intrusion, while the heat of the mound keeps the eggs warm. Mallee fowl (*Leipoa ocellata*) from Australia create a natural incubator for their eggs by burying them in a mound where the natural warmth generated by decaying vegetation means that the chicks eventually hatch on their own and dig themselves out.

Other birds, including members of the cuckoo family (Cuculidae), simply lay and abandon their eggs in the nests of other species. The foster parents-to-be cannot, apparently, detect the difference between their own eggs and those of the intruder, and proceed to incubate it with the others. The foster chick is subsequently fed and nurtured after hatching.

Birds that nest on the ground, such as the stone curlew (*Burhinus oedicnemus*), are especially vulnerable to predators and rely heavily on their drab plumage as camouflage. Skylarks (*Alauda arvensis*) have another means of protecting their nest site – they hold one wing down and pretend to be injured, to draw a predator away.

Below: Camouflage is important for all ground-nesting birds, irrespective of their size, as shown here by an incubating emu (Dromaius novaehollandiae). The coloration of these birds provides them with some protection when they are at their most vulnerable.

HATCHING AND REARING CHICKS

Birds are vulnerable to predators when breeding, especially when they have young in the nest. The chicks must be fed frequently, necessitating regular trips to and from the nest, which makes it conspicuous. The calls of the young birds represent a further danger, so the breeding period is often short.

Most birds incubate their eggs to keep them sufficiently warm for the chicks to develop inside. Larger eggs are less prone to chilling during incubation than small eggs, because of their bigger volume. In the early stages of the incubation period, when the nest may be left uncovered while the adult birds are foraging for food, eggs can withstand a lower temperature. Temperature differences also account for the fact that, at similar altitudes, incubation periods tend to be slightly longer in temperate areas than in tropical regions.

The eggshell may appear to be a solid barrier but in fact contains many pores, which are vital to the chick's well-being. These tiny holes allow water vapour and carbon dioxide to escape from the egg, and oxygen to enter it to reach the embryo.

Incubation

The incubation period often does not start until more than one egg has been laid, and sometimes not until the entire clutch has been completed. The interval between the laying of one egg and the next varies – finches lay every

Below: A fertile chicken's egg, showing the development of the embryo through to hatching. 1. The fertilized egg cell divides to form a ball of cells that gradually develops into an embryo. 2. The embryo develops, nourished by the yolk sac. 3. The air space at the rounded end of the egg enlarges as water evaporates. 4. The chick is almost fully developed and ready to hatch. 5. The chick cuts its way out, and its feathers dry off.

day, whereas gannets may lay only one egg every six days. If incubation does not start until egg-laying has finished, the chicks will all be of a similar size when they hatch, which increases their overall chances of survival.

The cock and hen may share incubation duties, as in the case of most pigeons and doves, or just one member of the pair may incubate. This is usually the hen, but there are exceptions. For example, with emus

Above: Breeding in one of the coldest places on Earth means that emperor penguins (Aptenodytes forsteri) can lay only a single egg, which they incubate on top of their feet, where special blood vessels help to warm it. After hatching, the chick is carried here too.

(*Dromaius novaehollandiae*) and other large flightless birds, it is the male who incubates the eggs and cares for the chicks. Anis (*Crotophaga*), of America, breed communally, and all members of the group share the task of incubation.

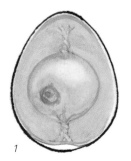

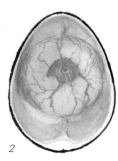

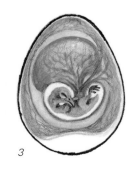

1   2   3   4   5

Early feathering

Most young birds have a coating of down feathering, which helps to insulate their bodies and keeps them warm, especially when they are not being brooded. Once their juvenile plumage emerges, however, it is usually duller in appearance than that of the adult birds. This helps to make them more inconspicuous during the vulnerable period after leaving the nest. Fledglings often resemble hens at first, in terms of their overall coloration, and it can take cock birds several years to acquire full adult plumage over a number of successive moults. Other birds more or less resemble adults from an early age.

Below: The soft, silky plumage of this young northern hawk owl (Surnia ulula) is actually similar in colour to the coat of adult birds. However, the white barring across the body will become more distinctive with age.

Hatching

Incubation periods vary among bird species, ranging from as few as 11 days in the case of cowbirds (*Molothrus*), to over 80 days in some albatrosses (Diomedeidae). Before hatching, the chick uses the egg tooth on the tip of its upper bill to cut through the inner membrane into the air space at the blunt end of the shell, which forms as water evaporates from the egg. The chick starts to breathe atmospheric air for the first time. About 48 hours later, it breaks through the shell to emerge from the egg.

Chicks hatch out at various stages of development, and are accordingly able to leave the nest sooner or later.

Species that remain in the nest for some time after hatching, including parrots (Psittaciformes) and finches (Fringillidae), hatch in a blind and helpless state and are entirely dependent on their parents at first. Birds in this group are known as nidicolous. If not closely brooded, they are likely to become fatally chilled. In contrast, species that leave the nest soon after hatching, known as nidifugous, emerge from the egg and are able to move around on their own at this stage. They can also see, and feed themselves almost immediately. The offspring of many game birds such as pheasants, as well as waterfowl and waders, are nidifugous, which gives them a better chance of survival, as they can run to escape from predators. Young waterfowl cannot take safely to the water at first, however, because they lack the oil from the preen gland above the base of the tail to water-proof their feathers.

Rearing and fledging

Many adult birds offer food to their offspring, even some nidifugous species. This can be a particularly demanding period, especially for small birds that have relatively large broods. Great tits (*Parus major*), for example, must supply their offspring with huge quantities of insects. They typically feed their chicks up to 60 times an hour, as well as keeping the nest clean.

Young birds usually leave the nest from about 12 to 30 days after hatching. However, some species develop much more slowly. Albatross chicks are particularly slow developers, spending up to eight and a half months in the nest.

When they first leave the nest, many young birds are unable to fly, simply because their flight feathers are not fully functional. If these feathers are not fully unfurled from the protective sheaths in which they emerged, they cannot function effectively. The strength of the wing muscles also needs to be built up, so it is not uncommon for young birds to rest on the sides of the nest, flapping their wings occasionally, before finally taking to the air for the first time. Chicks that

Above: A pair of red-headed tits (Aegithalos concinnus). As with related species, their young will leave the nest before they are able to fly effectively. Juveniles remain hidden in vegetation and are still fed by their parents during these critical early days after fledging.

are unable to fly immediately on fledging remain reliant on the adults, especially the cock, for food until they become fully independent.

For some young seabirds, fledging is a particularly hazardous process. From their cliff-ledge nests, they may simply flop down on to the water, where they are at risk from drowning unless able to master swimming skills. If they get swept out to sea, they may be caught by predators such as killer whales.

Below: The chicks of some finches such as this Australian Gouldian finch (Chloebia gouldiae) have fluorescent spots around their mouths as young nestlings, a feature that helps the parents to feed them quickly and easily during visits to the nest. These spots soon disappear as the chicks grow older.

SURVIVAL

The numbers of a particular species of bird can vary significantly over time, affected by factors such as the availability of food, climate, disease and hunting. When the reproductive rate of a species falls below its annual mortality rate, it is in decline, but this does not mean it will inevitably become extinct.

For many birds, life is short and hazardous. Quite apart from the risk of predation, birds can face a whole range of other dangers, from starvation and disease through to either deliberate human persecution or inadvertent interference. The reproductive rate is higher and the age of maturity lower in species that have hazardous lifestyles, such as blue tits (*Parus caeruleus*). These species often breed twice or more each year in rapid succession.

Rising and falling numbers

Some birds have a reproductive cycle that is geared to allow them to increase their numbers rapidly under favourable conditions. In Australia, for example, budgerigars (*Melopsittacus undulatus*) multiply rapidly when the rains come. Rainfall not only ensures the rapid growth of grasses that form the basis of their diet, but also fills the water-holes in the arid interior of the continent where these parakeets are found. During periods of drought, however, when food and water become

Below: Galah cockatoos (Eolophus roseicapillus) have not just benefited from increased availability of food and water in their natural habitat thanks to agriculture, but they have also adapted to other changes in the environment too, such as roosting together on this aerial.

Above: A stork scavenges for food around a dried-up riverbed. Birds such as these will not breed during the more arid times of year, when there are fewer feeding opportunities.

much harder for these nomadic birds to find, the population plummets. But it can grow again rapidly when conditions become more favourable.

Regular fall-offs in populations can occur on a cyclical basis, as shown by snowy owls (*Nyctea scandiaca*), which inhabit Arctic tundra north of several continents, including Asia. As major consumers of lemmings (an adult may eat more than three per day), a rise in the number of these small mammals will prompt a boom in the snowy owl population, as more chicks are reared successfully on a plentiful diet. If lemming populations decline, owls are forced to spread out over a much

wider area than normal in search of food, and their breeding success plummets accordingly. Later they gradually increase again as the lemming population recovers.

Group living

Birds that live in flocks find mates more easily than other birds, and group life also offers several other advantages, including the safety of numbers. An aerial predator such as a hawk will find it harder to recognize and target individuals in a flying mass of birds, although stragglers are still likely to be picked off.

Coloration can also increase the safety of birds in flocks. In Florida, USA, there used to be feral budgerigar flocks made up of multicoloured individuals. The different colours reflected the diversity of morphs that developed as a result of breeding in captivity. Today, however, green is by far the predominant colour in such flocks, as it is in genuine wild flocks, simply because predators found it much easier to pick off individuals of other colours. Greater numbers of the

green budgies survived to breed and pass on their genes to their descendants, and so green became the dominant colour in the feral flocks.

Group living also means that when the flock is feeding and at its most vulnerable, there are extra eyes to watch out for predators and other threats. Within parrot flocks, birds take it in turns to act as sentinels, and screech loudly at any hint of danger.

Effects of humans

It is generally assumed that human interference in the landscape is likely to have harmful effects on avian populations. However, this is not always the case. The expansion of agriculture in countries such as Australia has resulted in the greater availability of water in what was formerly arid countryside. This, in turn, has enabled birds such as galahs (*Eolophus roseicapillus*), a type of cockatoo, to spread over a much wider area and reproduce so rapidly that they have reached plague proportions. Shooting has helped to control numbers of these birds, but, overall, galah populations have expanded in recent years because of changes brought by humans.

Other birds have benefited more directly from human intervention, as is the case with the common starling (*Sturnus vulgaris*). These birds have spread across Australia, following their introduction from Europe in the late 1800s.

Similarly, the common pheasant (*Phasianus colchicus*) is now native across most of Asia, thanks to human interest in these game birds, which are bred in large numbers for sport shooting. Many more survive than would otherwise be the case, thanks to the attention of gamekeepers who not only provide food, but also help to curb possible predators in areas where the birds are released.

Slow breeders

Birds that reproduce slowly, such as albatrosses (Diomedeidae) and cranes (Gruidae), are likely to be highly vulnerable to any changes in their

Above: A Brolga crane (Grus rubicunda). Long-lived, slow-breeding birds such as cranes are the least adaptable when faced with rapid environmental change of any kind.

surroundings, whether caused by human interference, climate change, disease, or other factors. Great concern has recently been focused on albatross numbers, which are declining worldwide. Many of these birds have been caught and drowned in fishing nets in recent years. Albatrosses are normally very long-lived and breed very slowly. Any sudden decline in their population is therefore likely to have devastating consequences that cannot easily be reversed.

Below: The blue-crowned pigeon (Goura cristata) is not a prolific species, unlike some members of its family, and typically lays clutches comprised of just a single egg.

CONSERVATION ISSUES AND MIGRATION

One of the difficulties in assessing the health of avian populations is that a number of species are only found in a particular area for part of the year. Some birds, notably from western Asia, migrate to parts of Europe and Africa for the winter months, while other species undertake more local migrations.

It is becoming clear that a significant number of avian species are in decline. The threats faced by birds are varied and complex, but many are linked to human intervention in, and destruction of, their habitats. The well-publicized, but ongoing, destruction of rainforest, particularly in parts of South-east Asia, is just one example of potentially devastating environmental change. Introduced predators, such as domestic cats, form another threat. It should be remembered that some of the world's most distinctive birds have evolved in relative isolation on islands. They are therefore extremely vulnerable to changes in their habitat, partly because their populations are so small. Cats have been responsible for wiping out a host of island species. Most famously,

Below: Swift parakeets (Lathamus discolor) are relatively short-distance migrants, flying across the Bass Strait to the island of Tasmania from the mainland of Australia every spring, and returning in the autumn.

the flightless Stephen Island wren (*Xenicus lyalli*), of New Zealand's waters, became extinct in 1894, after being hunted incessantly by the lighthouse-keeper's cat.

Hunting and pollution

Unregulated hunting of adult birds, eggs or young threatens a variety of species worldwide. The birds may be killed for their meat or feathers, or captured live and sold through the pet trade. In many countries, laws are now in place to protect rare species, but hunting and trading still go on illegally.

Overfishing is a related hazard facing seabirds, especially now that trawling methods have become so efficient. Global shortages of fish stocks are forcing fishermen to target fish that had previously been of little commercial value, but which are an important part of many seabirds' diets.

In agricultural areas, pesticides and herbicides sprayed on farmers' fields decimate bird populations by eliminating their plant or animal food supplies. Deliberate or accidental contamination of the soil, air or water by industrial chemicals is another hazard, while other ocean birds fall victim to dumped toxins and oil spills.

Climate change

In the near future, global warming caused by increased emissions of carbon dioxide and other gases is likely to impact on many bird habitats, and will almost certainly adversely affect birds' food supplies. If plants or other foods become unavailable in an area, birds must adapt their feeding habits or face extinction. As temperatures rise, the melting of the polar ice caps will threaten seabird populations by destroying their traditional nesting areas. Rising sea levels will also threaten low-lying wetlands favoured by wading birds.

Above: A Bali starling (Leucopsar rothschildi), also known as the Rothschild's mynah, wearing an identification ring. A means of monitoring the actions of birds is vital when assessing the type of threats facing them.

Role of captive breeding

Preserving habitat is the best and most cost-effective way to ensure the survival of all birds within a particular ecosystem. A worldwide network of national parks and reserves now helps to protect at least part of many birds' habitats. In addition, conservationists are increasingly opting for a variety of more direct measures to safeguard the future of particular species, such as launching special captive-breeding programmes. In these schemes, national governments may work in conjunction with private breeders to improve the long-term survival chances of some of its avian life under threat. New Zealand's red-fronted parakeet (*Cyanoramphus novaezelandiae*) is one bird to benefit from this type of monitoring and protection. Zoos are co-operating in similar programmes, and establishing "studbooks" (which hold vital data on endangered species in captivity, partly to avoid harmful pairings of closely-related stock) for a

Above: The great hornbill (Buceros bicornis) *of Asia is just one of a number of endangered species that are now subject to internationally co-ordinated captive-breeding programmes, designed to boost its survival prospects.*

wide variety of birds from a specific region, ranging from endangered parrots to rare hornbills.

Reintroduction programmes

Breeding endangered species is relatively easy compared with the difficulties of reintroducing a species to an area of its former habitat. The cost of such reintroduction programmes is often very high. Staff are needed not only to look after the aviary stock and rear the chicks, but also to carry out habitat studies. These assess the dangers that the birds will face after release and pinpoint release sites. The released birds must then be monitored, which may include fitting them with radio transmitters.

Working with local people and winning their support is essential to the long-term success of conservation programmes. In the case of the rare Bali starling (*Leucopsar rothschildi*), visitors to this Indonesian island are being encouraged to visit the reserve where the surviving population of this species can be found. This brings in foreign currency for the local community, and also raises the international profile of the efforts being made to save this critically-endangered species.

Migration

The best-known form of migration is seasonal, where birds travel between summer and winter homes to avoid extremes of climate and ensure good food supplies. These regular journeys along specific routes are different from so-called irruptions, where flocks of birds appear unexpectedly in an area, usually encouraged by food supplies.

A third type of movement is more specific to birds living in Australia's arid interior, where conditions can be especially harsh. Many parakeets found in this region, including budgerigars (*Melopsittacus undulatus*), have a nomadic existence, moving throughout the region, from one area to another, in a seemingly random fashion. They may disappear from a location for many years, only to return again quite unexpectedly. Their arrival often portends that rain is imminent.

Navigation

Birds use both learned and instinctive cues to orientate themselves when migrating. Young birds of many species, such as swans, learn the route by flying in the company of their elders. However, some young birds set out on their own and reach their destinations successfully without the benefit of experienced companions, navigating by instinct alone. Birds such as swifts (Apopidae) fly mainly during daytime, whereas others, including ducks (Anatidae), migrate at night, when temperatures are cooler. Many birds fly direct to their destination, but some may detour and break their journey to obtain food and rest.

Experiments have shown that birds orientate themselves using the position of the sun and stars, as well as by following familiar landmarks. They also use the Earth's magnetic field to find their position, and thus do not get lost in cloudy or foggy weather, when the sky is obscured. The way in which these factors come together, however, has yet to be fully understood.

Monitoring avian populations

Much of what we know about the movements and lifespan of birds has originated from banding studies carried out by ornithologists. The band placed on the bird's leg allows the ringed individual to be identified when it is recovered. The rings themselves are made of lightweight aluminium, and record the date of banding. This method is not without its problems, however, as a high proportion of the ringed birds are never recovered. Newer tracking methods, such as radar, are becoming increasingly adept at recording birds' movements.

Below: Overfishing and pollution such as oil spills are hazards faced by many seabirds.

BEHAVIOUR

The study of bird behaviour, or avian ethology as it is known, is a very broad field. Some patterns of behaviour are common to all birds, whereas other actions are very specific, just to a single species or even to an individual population. Interpreting behaviour is easier in some cases than in others.

All bird behaviour essentially relates to various aspects of survival, such as avoiding predators, obtaining food, finding a mate and breeding successfully. Some behaviour patterns are instinctive, while others develop in certain populations of birds in response to particular conditions. The way in which birds behave is therefore partly influenced by their environment, as well as being largely instinctual.

Age, too, plays a part in defining behaviour, since young birds often behave in a very different way from

Above: The posture a bird adopts while sunbathing can appear to indicate distress, as is the case with this Eurasian blackbird (Turdus merula), which is resting with its bill open and wings outstretched.

the adults. Some forms of bird behaviour are relatively easy to interpret, while others are a great deal more difficult to explain.

Garden birds

One of the first studies documenting birds' ability to adapt their behaviour in response to changes in their environment involved blue tits (*Parus caeruleus*) in Britain. The study showed that certain individuals learned to use their bills to tap through the shiny metallic foil covers on milk bottles to reach the milk. Other blue tits followed their example, and in certain areas householders with milk deliveries had to protect their bottle tops from the birds.

The way in which birds have learned to use various types of garden feeders also demonstrates their ability to modify their existing behaviour in response to new conditions when it benefits them. A number of new feeders on the market designed to thwart squirrels from stealing the food

exploit birds' ability to adapt in this way. The birds have to squeeze through a small gap to reach the food, just as they might enter the nest. Once one bird has been bold enough to enter in this fashion, others observe and soon follow suit.

Preening

Although preening serves a variety of functions, the most important aspect is keeping the feathers in good condition. It helps to dislodge parasites and removes loose feathers, particularly during moulting. It also ensures that the plumage is kept waterproof by spreading oil from the preen gland at the base of the tail.

Preening can be a social activity too. It may be carried out by pairs of males and females during the breeding season, or among a family group.

Aggression

Birds can be surprisingly aggressive towards each other, even to the point of sometimes inflicting fatal injuries. Usually, however, only a few feathers are shed before the weaker individual backs away, without sustaining serious injury. Conflicts of this type can break out over feeding sites or territorial disputes. The risk of aggressive outbreaks is greatest at the onset of breeding, when the territorial instincts of cock birds are most aroused. Despite their popular image as symbols of peace, pigeons can be surprisingly aggressive birds on occasion, using their wings and bills to maim their opponent during often ferocious combat.

Below: This greater frigatebird (Fregata minor) of Australia and southern Asia will inflate its throat sac to deter aggressive rivals at a nesting site. This is a ploy to make the bird seem larger than it is.

This behaviour is seen in a variety of birds, ranging from parrots to finches. Some parrots perform mutual preening throughout the year, which reinforces the pair bond. In some species of psittaculid parakeets, however, such as the Alexandrine (*Psittacula eupatria*), the dominant hen allows her mate to preen her only when she is in breeding condition, in which case preening may be seen as a prelude to mating.

Bathing

Preening is not the only way in which birds keep their plumage in good condition. Birds often bathe to remove dirt and debris from their plumage. Small birds wet their feathers by lying on a damp leaf during a shower of rain, in an activity known as leaf-bathing. Other birds immerse themselves in a pool of water, splashing around and ruffling their feathers.

Some birds, especially those found in drier areas of the world, prefer to dust-bathe, lying down in a dusty hollow known as a scrape and using fine earth thrown up by their wings to absorb excess oil from their plumage. Then, by shaking themselves thoroughly, followed by a period of preening, the excess oil is removed.

Sunbathing

Sunbathing may be important in allowing birds to synthesize Vitamin D3 from the ultraviolet rays in sunlight, which is vital for a healthy skeleton. This process can be achieved only by light falling on the bird's skin, which explains why birds ruffle their plumage at this time. Some birds habitually stretch out while sunbathing, while others, such as many pigeons, prefer to rest with one wing

Right: An Anderson's bulbul (Pycnonotus xanthorrhous), poised to sing. The vocal sound is produced in the syrinx, at the base of the trachea, and involves the compression of air by muscles lining the body wall – hence the taut, rather strained appearance of the bulbul as it prepares to vocalize. Singing in birds is subject to hormonal control, and becomes more pronounced at the start of the breeding period. Young cock birds rarely develop their call until they approach sexual maturity.

raised, leaning over at a strange angle on the perch. Vasa parrots (*Coracopsis*), found on the island of Madagascar, frequently behave in this fashion, although sunbathing is generally not common in this group of birds.

Maintaining health

Some people believe that when birds are ill, they eat particular plants that have medicinal properties, but this theory is very difficult to prove. One form of behaviour that does confer health benefits has been documented, however: it involves the use of ants. Instead of eating these insects, some birds occasionally rub them in among their feathers. This causes the ants to release formic acid, which acts as a potent insecticide, killing off lurking parasites such as mites and lice. Jays (*Garrulus glandarius*) and also starlings (Sturnidae) and Eurasian blackbirds (*Turdus merula*) are among the birds that have been observed using insects in this way. Members of the crow family have also been seen perching on smoking chimney pots or above bonfires, ruffling their feathers and allowing the smoke to penetrate their plumage. The smoke is thought to kill off parasites in a process that confers the same benefits as anting.

Above: Many but not all members of the parrot family, such as this greater sulphur-crested cockatoo (Cacatua galerita), are able to use their feet to hold items of food, in a similar way to human hands. Studies have revealed that individual birds may actually be right-footed or left-footed in this respect.

Below: When birds rest, they typically fold their head back between the wings, as shown by this pelican (Pelecanus), but remain alert and quick to react to any potential danger.

CLASSIFICATION

The way in which different birds are grouped is known as classification. This is not only helpful in terms of distinguishing individual species and those that are closely related, but it also enables wider assessments of relationships between larger groups to be made.

Interest in how best to group birds into distinct categories is nothing new. It dates back nearly 2,500 years to the ancient Greeks, when an early method of classification was developed by the philosopher Aristotle. He sought to group living creatures on the basis of differences in their lifestyles, rather than on the basis of anatomical distinctions, which are favoured today. The first modern attempt to trace relationships between birds was made by Sir Francis Willoughby, in a book entitled *Ornithologia,* published in 1676. Willoughby saw the need for what was essentially an identification key that would enable readers to find an unknown bird by means of special tables devised for this purpose.

Above: The nominate subspecies of blue bonnet (Psephotus haematogaster haematogaster), *or "yellow-vented" type.*

Willoughby's work concentrated solely on birds, and it was a Swedish botanist, Carl von Linné (also known as Linnaeus), who devised the system of classification for all living things that is still used today, and known as the Linnean System. Linné relied primarily on the physical similarities between living organisms as the basis for grouping them, laying the foundations for the science of classification, which is now known as systematics. He refined this approach through a series of new editions of his classic work *Systema Naturae,* which was first published in 1735.

Linné's system operates through a series of ranks, creating what is sometimes described as a hierarchic method. Starting from a very general base, the ranks become increasingly specific, splitting into smaller groups,

Above: The bright red plumage on the belly of the red-vented blue bonnet (Psephotus haematogaster haematorrhous) *is more extensive than that of the yellow-vented race.*

until, finally, individual types of birds can be identified. An advantage of this system is that new species can be fitted easily into the existing framework.

New advances

While Linné and successive generations of taxonomists relied on physical similarities, the use of DNA analysis is currently transforming our understanding of the natural world. By comparing sequences of the genetic material DNA, it is possible for ornithologists to investigate which birds share DNA sequences that suggest a close relationship. This method of study is set to revolutionize taxonomy and is already leading to numerous revisions of the existing classification of birds.

How the system works

Birds, as animals, belong to the Kingdom Animalia, and, since they have backbones, are members of the phylum Chordata, which includes all vertebrates. The class Aves is the first

Above: The green plumage of the African race of ringnecked parakeet (Psittacula krameri krameri) tends to be of a more yellowish shade, and the bill is dark.

describing it in 1758. His method is sometimes known as the trinomial system, reflecting the fact that the name of the subspecies is made up of three parts.

What's in a name?

Even the choice of scientific names is not random. They often give an insight into a bird's appearance or distribution, using descriptions derived from Latin. The name *pacific*, in the case of the white-necked heron (*Ardea pacific*), for example, indicates this bird's love of swampy haunts close to the Pacific Ocean, notably on the east coast of Australia. In a few instances, the species' description features a person's name, for example *Chloebia gouldiae* – the Gouldian finch – which the noted naturalist and explorer John Gould named after his wife, Elizabeth, because of its beauty.

In order to be formally recognized as a species, an example of the bird concerned, known as the "type specimen", has to be held in a museum collection, where a detailed description of its characteristics is written up as part of the identification process.

Below: Subtle but consistent differences in coloration allow subspecies to be told apart. This is the Indian race of the ringnecked parakeet (Psittacula krameri manillensis), which boasts a brighter bill and greener coat.

division at which birds are separated from other vertebrates such as mammals. Birds alone comprise this major grouping, which is subdivided into smaller categories called orders. It is then a matter of tracking an individual species down through the various ranks of classification. For example, the classificatory breakdown of the blue bonnet is as follows:

Order: Psittaciformes
Family: Psittacidae
Genus: *Psephotus*
Species: *Psephotus haematogaster*
Subspecies: *Psephotus haematogaster haematogaster*; *P. h. haematorrhous*; *P. h. pallescens*; *P. h. narethae*.

If you are unsure where you are in the ranking, the way in which the names are written gives a clear indication. The names of orders end in "-formes", while family names terminate with "-idae". At or below genus level, all names are italicized, with the genus comprising one or more species. The scientific name of a species always consists of two descriptions, with the genus name being written first. Species are the basic fundamental level in the taxonomic tree, enabling particular types of birds to be named individually. Members of a particular species generally identify with each other and do not normally interbreed with other species. However, if interbreeding does occur, the resulting offspring are known as hybrids.

At the most specific level of the taxonomic tree are subspecies: closely related forms of the same species that are nevertheless distinct enough to be identified separately. These are often defined on the basis of their size, and also because of marked differences in coloration. In the case of the blue bonnet (*Psephotus haematogaster*), the nominate form (meaning the first form to be recognized) is *Psephotus haematogaster haematogaster*, which is distinguished by the repetition of the "trivial" name, *haematogaster*. The red-vented species carries the name *P. h. haematorrhous*, an abbreviated label that indicates its subtle differences in coloration from the nominate relative.

It was Linné himself who devised this method of distinguishing between such closely related individuals, first

DIRECTORY
OF BIRDS

Nowhere else in the world is there such a striking division between avian distributions as there is in this region. Although some of the birds occurring on the Asiatic mainland are also found further west in Europe, there is a very clear split in avian distributions off the coast of the Asian continent. Many of the species that inhabit the islands to the east and south, such as cockatoos, are restricted to this region, and do not occur on the mainland. There can be seasonal movements to some of these islands, however, with birds migrating southwards in Asia. The avifauna of New Zealand is particularly unusual, as birds have evolved here in the absence of mammalian predators over the course of many millions of years. While the dominant avian group – the giant moas – is now extinct, a number of other bizarre birds, such as the flightless kiwi, are still to be found on these islands.

Above from left: Rainbow lorikeet (Trichoglossus haematodus), *sulphur-crested cockatoo* (Cacatua sulphurea), *great hornbill* (Buceros bicornis).

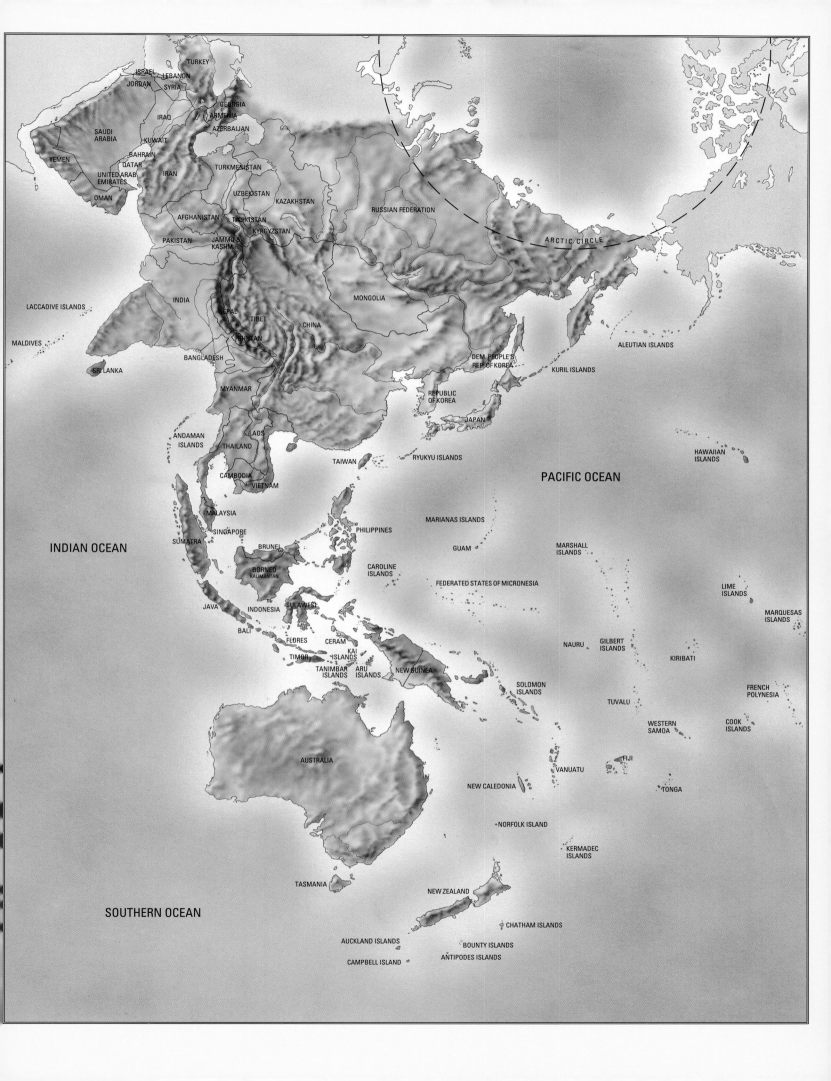

SEABIRDS

Many of the seabirds found in Asiatic and Australian waters have a wide distribution, which can be pan-global, often extending around the southern oceans and sometimes even further afield. Birds such as albatrosses are well adapted to spending virtually their entire lives on the wing, even to the extent of scooping their food from the surface of the sea and sleeping on the wing as they glide.

Red-billed tropic bird

Phaethon aethereus

These sleek, elegant birds swoop down from their cliff-top roosts and out over the oceans, catching their food by diving into the sea. The red-billed is the largest of the tropic birds. Their elegant, long, streaming white tail distinguishes them from the red-tailed tropic bird (*P. rubricauda*) which ranges further across the Indo-Pacific ocean to the south and also has paler, whitish wings. The bill of the Indian Ocean population of these tropic birds is less brightly coloured, serving to distinguish them from others of the species occurring elsewhere in the world. Islands rather than mainland areas are favoured breeding sites, as their position means that the birds will be in less danger from their predators.

Above: Red-billed tropic birds nest in crevices in the ground.

Identification: Predominantly white with a black streak running through the eyes. Black is clearly visible on the primary flight feathers at the ends of the wings. Black streaking runs over the back and rump down to the base of the tail. Tail streamers are longer in the cock bird than the hen. Bill reddish-orange with black edging.

Distribution: Ranges widely through the Red Sea, Gulf of Aden and the Persian Gulf. Other populations occur in the Caribbean as well as the southern Atlantic and the eastern Pacific oceans.
Size: 105cm (41in), including streamers up to 55cm (22in) in length.
Habitat: Tropical and subtropical seas.
Nest: Rocky crevice or hollow on the ground.
Eggs: 1, pinkish with darker markings.
Food: Mainly fish and squid. Sufficiently agile to catch flying fish.

Masked booby

Blue-faced booby *Sula dactylatra*

Distribution: This bird is pan-tropical – both north and south of the Equator – as it is found right around northern Australia.
Size: 92cm (36in).
Habitat: Sea.
Nest: On the ground or bare rock on cliff.
Eggs: 2, bluish white.
Food: Mainly fish.

Island habitats are favoured by the masked booby, allowing these birds to fly long distances out over the sea in search of prey, stopping off to rest on the islands as they do so. They catch fish by plunging into the middle of a shoal, swimming well underwater to achieve a catch. Apart from fish, other marine creatures, such as squid, feature less prominently in their diet. They live in colonies and individuals may sometimes be badly harried by frigate birds (*Fregata* species), which rob the masked boobies of their catch before they reach land. They lay their eggs on bare rock, and although two chicks may hatch, only one is likely to be reared successfully, unless food is freely available.

Identification: Large, white head, back and underparts. Dark areas around the eyes and the base of the bill. Black areas on the wings are apparent at rest and in flight. Tail feathers are black. The bill is yellowish in cock birds and greenish in hens. Legs and feet are greyish.

Wilson's storm petrel (*Oceanites oceanicus*): 19cm (7.5in)
Extends from Antarctica throughout the southern oceans into northern latitudes. Brownish overall, with a prominent white rump. Paler buff barring on the upper and underwing coverts. Sexes alike.

Sooty albatross (*Phoebetria fusca*): 89cm (35in)
Ranges across oceans from the west coast of Tasmania westwards almost as far as the Falkland Islands. A distinctive uniform shade of sooty black with a black bill. Its wings are long and pointed. Tail feathers are long and wedge-shaped. Sexes alike.

Fairy prion (*Pachyptila turtur*): 28cm (11in)
Found in three separate colonies in the southern oceans: one extends from south-east Australia to New Zealand. Grey crown, wings and back with white underparts and a dark tip to the tail. Blackish patterning across the wings. Sexes alike.

Streaked shearwater (white-fronted shearwater, *Calonectris leucomelas*): 48cm (19in)
Extends from eastern Asia from the Ryuku Islands and north-eastern Japan to Korea. Migrates south to Australia via New Guinea. Whitish underparts. Brown mottling on the sides of the head. Brown edging to the undersides of the wings. Upperparts are brown. Bill is silvery grey. Sexes alike.

Southern giant petrel
Macronectes giganteus

These aerial giants, with a wingspan of more than 2m (78in), and weighing as much as 5kg (11lb), can cover huge distances over the oceans of the southern hemisphere. They feed on the carcasses of marine mammals left on the shoreline, such as seals, as well as dead seabirds. They may be sighted close to trawlers, seeking offal and fish thrown overboard, which they scoop up from the sea's surface. These petrels nest on grassy islands in colonies of up to 300 pairs. The single chick develops slowly and may not fledge until it is nearly 20 weeks old. It is unlikely to breed for the first time until it is seven years old.

Identification: Brownish overall although darker on the lower underparts towards the vent. Paler greyish-brown head and neck. Bill yellow. The white morph of this species displays odd speckled brownish feathering on a white background. Hens smaller.

Distribution: Circumpolar in the southern ocean, occurring off the southern half of the Australian coastline and right around New Zealand.
Size: 99cm (39in).
Habitat: Sea.
Nest: Grassy mound or pile of stones.
Eggs: 1, white.
Food: Carrion.

Wandering albatross
Snowy albatross *Diomedea exulans*

Distribution: The range is circumpolar, extending from southern parts of Australia and New Zealand southwards. Also occurs on numerous smaller islands, such as Antipodes Island, all south-east of New Zealand.
Size: 135cm (53in).
Habitat: Sea.
Nest: Piles of mud and grass.
Eggs: 1, white with reddish-brown speckling.
Food: Mainly squid, but also fish, crustaceans and carrion.

As their name suggests, these albatrosses range widely over the southern oceans, often following ships and scavenging on galley scraps thrown overboard. They are also active hunters, however, scooping squid from the sea after dark, when these cephalopods come closer to the surface. Pairs separate at the end of the breeding period, but then some will reunite later on the breeding grounds. They breed only every second year because it takes nearly 40 weeks for a newly hatched chick to grow large enough to leave the nest.

Identification: Predominantly white. Black areas over much of the wings, although the areas closest to the body have only a black edging. There is often a pinkish area near the ear coverts, and there may be a greyish area on the crown. Bill is pink with a yellowish, hooked tip. Hens are slightly smaller, and may display a light greyish band around the chest and black on the edges of the tail.

PENGUINS, PELICANS AND OTHER COASTAL BIRDS

Although these birds are not closely related, they all depend on the marine environment for food in the form of fish or marine invertebrates. While some groups, such as plovers, have a broad distribution around the world, penguins in particular are confined to relatively cold areas of the southern hemisphere.

Rockhopper penguin

Eudyptes crysocome

Distribution: One population occurs in the southern ocean between Africa and Australia; one extends south from the southern coast of Australia; the third is on the eastern side of South America.
Size: 62cm (24.5in).
Habitat: Sea and close to the shoreline.
Nest: Made of grass and other available materials.
Eggs: 2, bluish white.
Food: Mainly krill. Some fish.

These penguins are so called because of the way they hop across land instead of walking. They live communally in rookeries, using their sharp bills to ward off gulls and other predatory birds that may land in their midst. Despite its relatively small size, the rockhopper is the most aggressive of all penguins. It is also one of the most adaptable, being found even in temperate areas. These penguins feed underwater, using their wings like flippers to steer themselves. If danger threatens, they swim towards the shore and leap out of the water on to the land with considerable force.

Identification: White underparts. Black head, flippers and tail although the ear coverts appear slightly paler. The bill is red, as are the irises. A line of golden plumage forms a crest towards the rear on each side of the head. Hens are smaller and have less stout bills.

Above: These ungainly hopping penguins are elegant swimmers.

Spot-billed pelican

Grey pelican *Pelecanus philippensis*

This particular species is thought to be the rarest member of the pelican family and its range is now greatly reduced. Indeed, it is extinct in the Philippines despite also being known as the Philippine pelican. The use of pesticides may have contributed to this decline, along with habitat changes. These large birds weigh about 5kg (11lb) and need to catch roughly a fifth of their body weight in food every day, so easy access to food is imperative to their survival. Widespread destruction of forests is also believed to have had an adverse effect on their numbers, as these pelicans require large trees in which to build their nests.

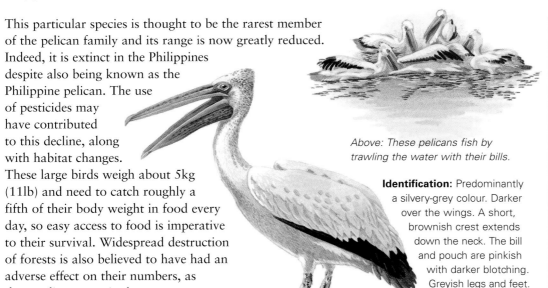

Above: These pelicans fish by trawling the water with their bills.

Identification: Predominantly a silvery-grey colour. Darker over the wings. A short, brownish crest extends down the neck. The bill and pouch are pinkish with darker blotching. Greyish legs and feet. Sexes are alike.

Distribution: South-east India and Sri Lanka east to Myanmar (Burma) and south-eastern parts of China. Overwinters further south reaching Sumatra and Java.
Size: 150cm (59in).
Habitat: Ranges from coastal bays to lakes.
Nest: Made of vegetation.
Eggs: 2–3, chalky white.
Food: Fish.

Greater frigate bird

Fregata minor

The frigate bird is an aerial hunter, scooping up its prey from the surface of the ocean, and is attracted by shoals of flying fish, and squid too. These birds are opportunistic when feeding, however, and will swoop over beaches where turtles nest to catch and eat the hatchling reptiles as they try to make for the relative safety of the sea. Frigate birds will also harry other sea-birds, causing them to drop their catches, which they then take themselves. The frigate bird breeds in colonies on remote islands. Their chicks develop very slowly and are cared for by both their parents for up to a year and a half after birth.

Above: The greater frigate bird inflates the throat sac for display purposes.

Identification: Dark overall with a bright red throat sac. Abdomen is black. Has a long, hooked bill and a streaming tail. Brownish wing bars on the upper side of the wings. An angular wing posture is evident in flight. The black areas of plumage have a glossy green suffusion when the light catches them. Sexes are similar but the hens are larger with a greyish white throat and white chest.

Distribution: Mainly in the Pacific, from the west coast of South America to the northern coast of Australia and southern Asia to East Africa. A smaller population also occurs in the south Atlantic.
Size: 105cm (41in).
Habitat: Islands and mangroves.
Nest: Platform of sticks.
Eggs: 1, chalky white.
Food: Mainly fish, some squid and carrion occasionally.

Royal penguin (*Eudyptes schlegeli*): 76cm (30in)
Distribution centred on Mocker Island, south of New Zealand and Campbell Island. Sometimes found on the southern coast of New Zealand. Crested, but with a distinctive white face. Black plumage on the crown, back and wings. Under-parts are white. Has a greyish band across the throat. Hens smaller, with a less robust bill.

King penguin (*Aptenodytes patagonicus*): 95cm (37in)
This penguin is almost circumpolar, breeding on sub-Antarctic and Antarctic islands. Has a black head with a relatively narrow orange collar around the side of the head. Upperparts are greyish. On the upper chest, underparts are white with an orange suffusion. Long bill which is pale red near the base of the lower mandible. Sexes are alike. These large penguins weigh up to 15kg (33lb).

Little penguin (fairy penguin; *Eudyptula minor*): 45cm (18in)
Found on southern coasts of Australia, extending from Perth and east to Tasmania, New Zealand and the Chatham Islands. Has dark greyish-black upperparts and white underparts. Dull pinkish black bill. Pink feet. Sexes alike. Weighing barely 1kg (2.2lb), this is the smallest of the penguins.

Crab plover (*Dromas ardeola*): 40cm (16in)
Confined to the Indian Ocean coastline. White body with areas of black feathering on the top and edges of the wing. Legs are greyish. Large, heavy, blackish bill is used for crushing crabs. Sexes alike. It is the only wader that nests in underground tunnels over 1.5m (5ft) in length.

Milky stork

Mycteria cinerea (E)

The name of these storks originates from the milky white shade of their plumage when they are in breeding condition. Milky storks have become much rarer through their range for a variety of reasons, which include habitat destruction. In Vietnam, the widespread use of defoliant chemicals in mangrove swamps during the Vietnam War is thought to have affected their numbers to the extent that there is only a single breeding colony left in the country. The largest remaining population occurs on the eastern part of the Indonesian island of Sumatra. There is some movement of these storks after breeding, which takes place during the dry season. They use their long bill to probe for food in often muddy water, grabbing fish and small vertebrates that come within reach.

Identification: Predominantly white, but has a bald, reddish area of skin over much of the face and a black patch by the base of the bill. The edge of the wings are blackish. Legs and feet are red and the bill is straw-coloured. Young birds have more extensive feathering on their heads and their bare skin is yellowish. Sexes alike.

Distribution: Scattered localities through South-east Asia, notably Vietnam, Malaysia, Sumatra, Java and Sulawesi.
Size: 100cm (39in).
Habitat: Coastal mudflats and mangroves.
Nest: Platform of sticks in a tree.
Eggs: 1–4, whitish.
Food: Fish and other vertebrates.

KINGFISHERS, CORMORANTS AND OTHER FISH-EATERS

The hunting strategies of this group of birds differ widely, but they are all well adapted to their environments. The way in which they have evolved in this respect is perhaps best illustrated by the collared kingfisher, which occurs in a huge number of different forms through its wide range.

Collared kingfisher

Mangrove kingfisher *Halcyon chloris*

More than 50 distinctive races of the collared kingfisher are recognized across its extensive distribution. Many of the most distinctive evolved in relative isolation on remote Pacific islands, such as New Britain – their white areas are heavily suffused with an orange shade. On the southern Mariana islands, however, the white plumage is more extensive, covering virtually the entire head apart from bluish-green stripes behind the eyes. The diet of these birds is equally variable, ranging from crabs to cicadas, snails and even small snakes. When nesting, the collared kingfisher is highly territorial although pairs will drive away intruders at any time of the year.

Distribution: Extends over a huge area from the Red Sea across southern Asia and the Pacific islands on to northern and eastern Australia.
Size: 25cm (11in).
Habitat: Coastal areas. Sometimes inland.
Nest: Tree hole or an arboreal termite mound.
Eggs: 2–5, white.
Food: Invertebrates, crustaceans and small vertebrates.

Identification: Highly variable appearance depending on the subspecies, although the wings are invariably greenish blue with bright blue edges. Underparts are generally white and the collar is white as well. Many races have a greenish-blue crown with a black stripe running through the eyes. The beak is black, with a distinct paler base to the lower bill. Sexes are alike.

Little pied cormorant

Phalacrocorax melanoleucos

Distribution: Extends from eastern Indonesia to the Solomon Islands and New Caledonia, and south to Australia and New Zealand.
Size: 65cm (26in).
Habitat: Coastal areas and inland waters.
Nest: Platform of sticks usually with trees nearby, which will be used for nesting purposes.
Eggs: 3–5, pale bluish.
Food: Fish and other aquatic creatures.

The appearance of these cormorants varies noticeably through the range. The New Zealand race (*P. m. brevirostris*), for example, displays a variable amount of white plumage on the underparts. These cormorants obtain their food by diving, seeking not just fish but also amphibians, crustaceans and other invertebrates, with the prey varying according to the cormorant's habitat. Although they are occasionally seen in loose groups, little pied cormorants tend to fish independently and may even take up residence in public parks where they feed heavily on goldfish in the ponds.

Identification: Distinctive appearance. Has a predominantly white head with black plumage to the crown area that extends down the back of the neck. Underparts may be entirely white or black, depending on the race. Has a long black tail and a small crest on the head. The bill is yellowish. Feet and legs are black. Sexes alike.

Brown booby

White-bellied booby *Sula leucogaster*

These boobies hunt a variety of fish relatively close to the shoreline, so usually they dive into the water from a low height, hitting the surface at an angle rather than entering vertically. This means that they penetrate the water less deeply. They are effective underwater swimmers, using their webbed feet and their wings to help them. The brown booby has an interesting relationship with its masked relative (*S. dactylatra*) when their distribution overlaps. They sometimes harry masked boobies for food in flight, stealing their catch. Rare mixed pairings between these two species have given rise to hybrid offspring.

Identification: Blackish head and upper chest, with browner suffusion to the feathers of the back, wings and tail. The underparts are white and the feet are yellow. Has a powerful bill which is bluish at the base, becoming dull yellow towards the tip. Hens are larger in size.

Distribution: Extends from the western Pacific to the east coast of Africa. Also present in the Atlantic, the Caribbean, and the western coast of Central America.
Size: 74cm (29in).
Habitat: Inshore waters.
Nest: Hollow on the ground.
Eggs: 2, bluish white.
Food: Fish.

Silver gull (*Larus novaehollandiae*): 43cm (17in)
Extends from the coast of Ethiopia around the Asiatic coastline south to mainland Australia and Tasmania. Also occurs as far east as New Caledonia. Has a predominantly white and silvery-grey back, with black evident on the flight feathers. Orange-red ring around the eyes. Bill red, as are the legs. Sexes alike.

Whiskered tern (*Chlidonias hybrida*): 27cm (11in)
Widely distributed on shores from southern Africa to Asia, including the Indonesian islands and New Guinea, south to Australia. It is sometimes seen as a vagrant in Tasmania. Cocks in breeding condition have a black cap on the head and the rest of their body is grey apart from white areas on the sides of the face. Cap becomes speckled outside the breeding season, when underparts are white. Wings are grey. Sexes are alike.

Black-naped tern (*Sterna sumatrana*): 35cm (14in)
Found on islands and coastal areas throughout the Indian and Pacific Oceans south to northern Australia. Predominantly white, with a strongly forked tail and a black area extending back from the eyes around the nape. Has silvery wings and a black bill. Sexes are alike.

Little black shag (*Phalacrocorax sulcirostris*): 65cm (26in)
Ranges from New Guinea westwards to Indonesia and then southwards to Australia, including Tasmania, and on to New Zealand. Occurs both in coastal and inland areas. Has black plumage, a black bill and black feet. Traces of white feathering above the eye are only evident during the breeding season. Sexes are alike.

Mangrove heron

Green-backed heron *Butorides striatus*

The great variation in the appearance of the mangrove heron has led to more than 30 distinctive races being recognized by taxonomists. It is not just differences in coloration that sets them apart, but also their size because the Australian races are larger than those from elsewhere. These herons are equally at home in saltwater areas, such as mangroves, as well as fresh-water lakes, although they prefer areas where there is dense cover as this enables them to keep their presence hidden. Their shy nature is also reflected in their feeding habits. The mangrove heron often prefers to seek food at night, if the tide is favourable.

Identification: Very variable, even between members of the same race. Blackish plumage on the crown. Underparts are often pinkish greyish with a white stripe down the centre of the body, but can range from light brown to grey. Usually a bare area of yellow skin is most conspicuous in front of the eyes. Wings dark. Sexes are generally alike.

Distribution: Pan-global: ranges from the Indian subcontinent through South-east Asia to northern and eastern parts of Australia.
Size: 48cm (19in).
Habitat: Shallow water.
Nest: Built of twigs in a tree or bush.
Eggs: 2–5, pale blue.
Food: Fish and other aquatic life, reptiles and mice.

WADING BIRDS

These birds are well equipped to forage in wetland areas, with their long legs enabling them to wade through the shallows easily, while also giving them a good field of vision to detect possible prey. A sharp bill and rapid reflexes make them formidable hunters of small aquatic creatures. They may also be encountered in fields close to stretches of water.

White-necked heron

Pacific heron *Ardea pacific*

The main distribution of these herons is centred on Australia. Although less common here, they also congregate in areas such as Irian Jaya in New Guinea. Following prolonged periods of rainfall, flooding means that these herons have greater feeding opportunities so populations can shift quite widely in search of flooded areas. They may be seen in coastal areas but prefer freshwater localities. White-necked herons breed in colonies of 20 or so pairs, building their nests in trees at least 15m (49ft) off the ground. Occasionally, much larger groups of as many as 150 pairs have been observed. They often nest in trees with other birds, such as spoonbills. Juvenile birds can be distinguished by greyish, rather than white, plumage on their head and neck.

Identification: The head and neck are white, and have slight black streaking in the centre of the lower throat and upper breast when out of breeding condition. Wings are blackish with a grey overlay. The underparts are blackish with white streaking. The bill, legs and feet are dark. Sexes alike.

Distribution: Found in southern New Guinea. Also present throughout Australia, apart from the central area.
Size: 106cm (41in).
Habitat: Shallow waters.
Nest: Platform of sticks.
Eggs: 3–4, pale blue.
Food: Small fish, vertebrates.

Cattle egret

Bubulcus ibis

Distribution: Exceedingly wide pan-global distribution. Asiatic race extends from southern and eastern parts of Asia into parts of Australia and New Zealand.
Size: 56cm (22in).
Habitat: Shallow waters and even relatively dry areas.
Nest: Sometimes in reedbeds, often on a platform above the ground.
Eggs: 2–5, pale blue.
Food: Invertebrates, amphibians and other small vertebrates.

The sharp bills of these egrets allow them to catch their quarry easily, although in urban areas they can often be seen scavenging around markets and in rubbish dumps. The Asiatic race (*B. i. coromandus*) is the largest and tallest of the three subspecies found worldwide. Banding studies have revealed that cattle egrets will fly long distances, with those birds occurring in north-eastern Asia moving south in the winter. Ringed birds have turned up as far afield as the Philippines. This tendency to roam widely has allowed these egrets to colonize many of the more remote islands in the Pacific. Indeed, distinct seasonal movements have even been recorded in Australia.

Identification: Pale buff coloration on the head and throat, extending down to the breast; also on the back and rump. The remainder of the plumage is white. There may be traces of white plumage around the yellow bill. The legs and feet are also yellow. Sexes alike.

Below: The egret's buff plumage is replaced largely by white during the breeding period for display purposes.

Sarus crane

Grus antigone

These large, long-lived birds pair for life, which can be for 30 years or more. They are easily spotted from some distance away in open, wet countryside, usually in pairs. In areas where food is plentiful, however, larger numbers of sarus cranes may occasionally gather together, with as many as 60 individuals recorded in one locality. These cranes are relatively fearless, often stalking among cattle in fields to pounce on small animals, such as frogs, that have been disturbed by the herd. In common with other species of cranes, their courtship involves a spectacular dancing ritual which is accompanied by loud calls.

Identification: Grey plumage, with a characteristic red head and long neck. Has an area of black plumage on the wings. The tertiaries drooping over the grey tail are pale, verging on white. Straight greenish, horn-coloured bill that tapers to a point. Legs are reddish and very long. Sexes alike.

Distribution: Ranges from the Indian subcontinent east and south across Cambodia and Laos, Vietnam as far as north-eastern Australia.
Size: 152cm (60in).
Habitat: Wetland areas, including paddy fields.
Nest: Platform of vegetation on the ground.
Eggs: 2, pinkish-white. May have brown markings.
Food: Invertebrates, fish, frogs, and some vegetable matter.

Plumed egret (*Egretta intermedia*): 72cm (28in)
Extends from New Guinea to eastern Indonesia and south to Australia. White body, with delicate plumes over the back and on the chest. The bill and the area around the eyes are yellow in the Asiatic race (*E. i. plumifera*). Top part of the legs are yellowish. The feet are greyish.Sexes alike.

Australasian bittern (brown bittern, *Botaurus poiciloptilus*): 76cm (30in)
Found in south-west and south-east Australia, including Tasmania, plus New Zealand, New Caledonia and the Loyalty Islands. Has white plumage on the throat and running down on to the neck. Brownish elsewhere but with black markings. The depth of coloration varies among individuals. Pale stripe above the eye. The bill and legs are pale yellow.

Black-necked stork (*Ephippiorhynchus asiaticus*): 137cm (54in)
Two populations: one is confined essentially to India; the other is in northern and eastern Australia. Glossy black plumage on the head and neck. The body is white apart from prominent black areas on the wings. Strong, powerful black bill. Legs and feet are red.

Straw-necked ibis (*Threskiornis spinicollis*): 76cm (30in)
Found in New Guinea and Australia apart from central and central-southern areas. Bare black head with white collar over much of the neck and buff area beneath. Rest of the upper breast area, back and wings are all greenish. Underparts white. Legs are red. Hens smaller.

Glossy ibis

Plegadis falcinellus

Groups of these ibises can be encountered in a wide range of environments, from rice fields to river estuaries, and they will often undertake extensive seasonal movements. They tend to feed by probing into the mud with the tips of their sensitive bills, enabling them to grab prey easily even if the water is muddy. They occasionally dip their heads under water when feeding, too. These birds may also use their long legs to pursue prey, such as snakes, on the ground. Pairs nest colonially. The nest site is located low over the water, so fledglings sometimes fall victim to crocodiles lurking nearby as they venture away from the nest.

Distribution: Wide. Extends from the Red Sea via northern India to the eastern coast of Asia. Also present in Australia, the Philippines and Indonesia.
Size: 66cm (26in).
Habitat: Shallow areas of water.
Nest: Platform of sticks, built above water.
Eggs: 2–6, deep green to blue.
Food: Invertebrates, plus crustaceans and small vertebrates.

Identification: Dark brown overall but with some white streaking on the head. The wings and rump are green. Legs and bill are dark. When not in breeding condition, they are a duller colour. Sexes are alike.

WATERFOWL

This group of birds has diversified to occupy a wide range of habitats and has adopted a correspondingly broad range of lifestyles, from grazing wetland areas to an almost entirely aquatic existence. Breeding habits vary, too, with some members of the group preferring to breed on the ground, while others choose the relative safety of tree hollows for their nest site.

Cape Barren goose

Cereopsis goose *Surpasses novaehollandiae*

Distribution: Found in parts of southern Australia, including Tasmania. Breeds in four main areas: the Furneaux islands, Spencer Gulf islands, islands of the Recherche Archipelago and off Wilson's Promontory.
Size: 99cm (39in).
Habitat: Pasture and open country.
Nest: Made of vegetation, built on the ground.
Eggs: 3–6, white.
Food: Grasses and sedges.

These geese live almost entirely on land, only taking to water as a last resort when danger threatens, or when, during the moult, they are unable to fly for a period. They breed on small islands, where they are relatively safe from disturbance, nesting among the tufts of grass and other vegetation which they browse using their strong bills. Male birds have a much louder call than hens, whose vocalisations have been described as pig-like grunts. They weigh up to 5.3kg (12lb) but are still powerful in flight, their wing beats being both shallow and fast.

Identification: A distinctive grey colour with a paler whitish area on the head. Tail is black. Some irregular darker spotting on the wings, most pronounced in young birds. Reddish legs with black feet. Greatly enlarged greenish-yellow cere encompassing the nostrils. Bill is black. Hens are smaller in size.

Above: Cape Barren geese graze in flocks on grass: they are highly sociable birds by nature.

Cotton pygmy goose

White pygmy goose *Nettapus coromandelianus*

These geese spend most of their time on the water, frequently favouring deep areas. They are most commonly observed in pairs or small groups, although they occasionally congregate in much greater numbers outside the breeding season. These geese feed by dabbling under the water, only diving down occasionally, and often choosing vegetation growing above the water's surface. When flushed out, they fly quite low and generally not very far. The breeding season begins at the onset of the rainy season. Pairs nest individually and tend to remain close to the water. In some parts of their range, most notably in Australia, the numbers of cotton pygmy geese have declined as the result of wetland drainage.

Identification: A black stripe runs from the bill over the top of the head. A black collar runs around the upper breast and this is intersected with an area of white plumage. Underparts are mainly pale grey and the wings are blackish. Female is duller: mainly grey with black eye stripe. When not in breeding plumage, cock birds resemble hens, apart from a larger, white area on the wing.

Distribution: India eastwards across Asia. Also in Indonesia and eastern Australia.
Size: 37cm (14in).
Habitat: Deep water with plant growth.
Nest: Tree hollows lined with down.
Eggs: 6–16, ivory white.
Food: Aquatic plants and invertebrates.

White-eyed duck

Australian hardhead *Aythya australis*

Although these pochards are usually only encountered in Australia, they do irrupt on occasion and can then be seen much further afield in countries as far apart as Java and New Zealand. It is thought that such behaviour is usually triggered by severe droughts. It is believed that the remote population on Banks Island originated as a result of an irruption of this kind, rather than from a deliberate human introduction, and these immigrants have successfully established a separate breeding population. In Australia, there has been a decline in the number of white-eyed ducks over recent years as a by-product of drainage schemes.

Identification: A rich chocolate-brown colour with white lower breast and belly. Has white plumage around the vent. Bill is greyish, with a light band and a black tip. Iris is whitish. Females are very similar, but have dark eyes and may be slightly lighter and browner overall. There is no eclipse plumage. Juvenile birds resemble females but have russet-brown feathering on the abdomen.

Distribution: Australia, apart from central and central-southern parts. Isolated colony on Banks Island.
Size: 59cm (23in).
Habitat: Large, well-vegetated lakes and marshes.
Nest: Platform of vegetation.
Eggs: 9–13, greenish-grey.
Food: Mainly plant matter, some invertebrates.

Chestnut-breasted shelduck (Australian shelduck, *Tadorna tadornoides*): 72cm (28in)
Occurs mainly in western and south-eastern parts of Australia, including Tasmania, in shallow stretches of water. Drakes have glossy dark green head and neck with a narrow white collar separating this area from the chestnut breast. The remainder of the body, apart from the chestnut rump, is dark. The broad white area in the wing is most visible in flight. Ducks are recognizable by white edging around the base of the bill and eyes. They have greyish-brown bodies in eclipse plumage.

Pacific black duck (*Anas superciliosa*): 61cm (24in)
Found in Indonesia, New Guinea and islands to the east, as well as Australia, New Zealand and neighbouring islands. The basic coloration varies from brown to black, with lighter scalloping on the feathers. Has green speculum in the wing. Dark crown, and an eye stripe with buff lines is evident on the face as well. The bill is greyish and the legs and feet are a yellowish-grey. Hens tend to have browner plumage on the upper-parts of the body.

Magpie goose (*Anseranas semipalmata*): 85cm (34in)
Present in southern New Guinea and northern Australia and extending down the east coast. The body is white apart from glossy, blackish plumage on the head and rear of the body. There is a swollen area on the crown of the head. The bare facial skin is reddish. The legs are a golden yellow. Hens are smaller, and the swollen area is less pronounced.

Lesser tree duck

Lesser whistling duck *Dendrocygna javanica*

This is the smallest of the tree ducks, and like other members of the group, it prefers to roost in trees at night rather than on the water. The breeding habits of the lesser tree duck are unusual because although it does sometimes nest on the ground, it usually prefers to choose a site in a suitable tree. Pairs tend to either adopt a tree hollow for this purpose or to take over an abandoned platform nest made from sticks that would have been constructed originally by herons or a bird of prey. Only at the northern edge of their current distribution do these birds head south in the winter. They used to occur in Japan, but, sadly, they were hunted to extinction in the early 20th century.

Distribution: From India and Pakistan eastwards across mainland Asia to China. Wide distribution across South-east Asia. Also south to Indonesian islands, including Java and Sumatra, and the island of Borneo.
Size: 40cm (16in).
Habitat: Shallow water edged with trees.
Nest: Either on the ground or in trees.
Eggs: 7–12, creamy white.
Food: Plant matter and aquatic snails.

Identification: Brownish, with a darker streak across the top of the head. Underparts are slightly pinkish. White area around the vent. Dark brown back and wings with lighter scalloping. Grey bill, legs and feet. Sexes alike.

FROGMOUTHS AND OWLS

These hunting birds are all cryptically coloured, with none of them displaying the bright plumage seen in the case of some woodland birds. Their hearing and keen vision help to alert them to the presence of possible prey. In spite of their popular image, however, not all owls are nocturnal hunters, with some being seen on the wing throughout the day rather than solely becoming active at dusk.

Large frogmouth

Batrachostomus auritus

These frogmouths seem to be rare on the Asiatic mainland, and so relatively little is known about their habits. What we do know is that they hunt off a perch, seeking invertebrates, such as grasshoppers or cicadas, which they swoop down on and seize in their bill. Large frogmouths have a very wide gape that allows them to feed easily. They are nocturnal creatures, hunting from dusk onwards. They are reminiscent of owls, in terms of cryptic coloration and calls.

Identification: These birds are much larger than other frogmouths. They have dark rufous-brown upperparts amd white spotting forms a collar around the back of the neck. There are both white spots on the wings and buff barring on the flight feathers. The throat and breast are similar in shade to the upperparts, with white spotting on the breast and buff plumage on the belly. Forward-pointing bristles mask the bill. The eyes are relatively large. Hens are duller in colour and smaller overall.

Distribution: Ranges from peninsular Thailand and through Malaysia to Sumatra and Borneo.
Size: 41cm (16in), making this species twice as large as other frogmouths.
Habitat: Lowland forest.
Nest: Pad of down on a tree.
Eggs: 1, white.
Food: Invertebrates.

Collared owlet

Glaucidium brodiei

These owlets are unusual members of the owl family in that they hunt during the day, and may be seen in the vicinity of open clearings. Their vocalizations are unusual too, consisting of a series of quite musical call notes. In spite of their small size, these birds are aggressive hunters, and can take birds and even lizards as large as themselves. Their strong feet and fearsome-looking talons enable them to hold down their prey with ease as they kill it with their strong bill. It is not unusual for these owlets to be mobbed by groups of other birds. The disturbance that results from the driving mob can provide a means of identifying the owlets' presence in an area.

Above: The spots on the back of the collared owlet's head resemble eyes. This serves to deter possible predators.

Identification: Greyish-brown barred plumage. Has lemon-yellow eyes and white eyebrows and throat area. The underparts are also whitish. Greenish-yellow feet. Hens larger in size.

Distribution: Ranges from the Himalayan region east to China and southwards through much of the Malay Peninsula, then on to parts of Sumatra and Borneo.
Size: 15cm (6in).
Habitat: Hill and mountain forests with clearings, ranging up to an altitude of around 3,200m (10,500ft).
Nest: Tree hollow. The owl either uses a natural hole or takes over a chamber created by a woodpecker or barbet.
Eggs: 3–5, white.
Food: Large invertebrates and small vertebrates.

Barred eagle owl

Malay eagle owl *Bubo sumatranus*

Hard to spot during the daytime, barred eagle owls frequently choose to roost in a concealed locality out of sight, well disguised by foliage, with their barred pattern of markings helping to provide them with additional camouflage. They are also not especially common, simply because pairs occupy large territories. These owls are thought to pair for life and will return annually to the same nest site, with pairs occurring in Sumatra and Java not infrequently choosing a large bird's nest fern (*Asplenium*), rather than a tree hollow.

Identification: Large, fairly horizontal tufts of feathers on the top of the head, directed to the sides, with white streaks above dark brown eyes. Barred blackish-brown and buff plumage, with a finer pattern of barring across the breast. Underparts whiter overall, but still with distinct barring. Bill and feet are a pale yellow. Hens may be larger.

Distribution: From southern Myanmar (Burma) and Thailand across the Malay Peninsula to Borneo, Sumatra, Java, Bali and adjacent islands.
Size: 46cm (18in).
Habitat: Tropical forests up to 1,600m (5,250ft).
Nest: Tree holes and ferns.
Eggs: 1, white.
Food: Invertebrates and smaller vertebrates.

Spotted wood owl (*Strix seloputo*): 47cm (18.5in)
Found across South-east Asia over the Malay Peninsula to coastal areas of Java. Also present on Palawan in the Philippines and may occur on Sumatra. Rufous-buff facial disc. No ear tufts. Brownish barring on the underparts, may have areas that are whitish to more definite shades of buff. Eyes brown. Bill greyish. Hens larger.

Brown hawk owl (*Ninox scutulata*): 32cm (13in)
Extends from the Indian subcontinent and South-east Asia to some Indonesian islands, Japan and the Philippines, then via the mainland to eastern Siberia. White underparts with brown streaking. Some subspecies may have underparts of lighter brown than the streaking. Brownish back and wings. Greyish-black bill. Hens are usually smaller.

Oriental bay owl (*Phodilus badius*): 33cm (13in)
Ranges across South-east Asia to Indonesia. Also present on Samar in the Philippines. An isolated population exists in south-west India and on Sri Lanka. Whitish facial disc, resembling a mask, with a speckled collar beneath. The wings are reddish-brown with speckling; underparts paler. A distinctive v-shaped frontal shield extends from between the eyes to the base of the yellow bill. Females are usually bigger.

Buffy fish owl (*Bubo ketupu*): 48cm (19in)
Extends from southern Myanmar (Burma) into Thailand, through the Malay Peninsula to various Indonesian islands. Predominantly brown back and wings. The underparts are a pale yellowish-brown. Unfeathered, pale yellowish legs. Yellow eyes and black bill. Females larger.

Mountain scops owl

Spotted scops owl *Otus spilocephalus*

Inhabiting relatively inaccessible areas such as deep ravines, these owls become active at dusk when they begin to hunt their invertebrate prey. Males occupy relatively small territories and sing regularly, even outside the breeding period, with their calls sounding like a double whistle. Hens call far less often with their single note being heard in response to that of the cock bird, before merging into it. Although little has been recorded about their hunting habits, it is thought these scops owls obtain at least some of their prey on the wing, with moths as well as beetles featuring significantly in their diet.

Identification: Quite a small size compared to other owls. Some regional variation in colour. White feathering runs along the upper part of each wing. Underparts are brownish and have white areas crossed by black marks that are said to resemble arrowheads. Bristles are apparent on the face. Yellow eyes. The bill is cream. Sexes are alike.

Distribution: Indian Himalayan region, parts of Nepal, Pakistan and Myanmar (Burma), to south-eastern China, Taiwan and south through the Malay Peninsula to Sumatra and Borneo.
Size: 18cm (7in).
Habitat: Humid upland areas of forest.
Nest: Tree holes, sometimes excavated by other birds.
Eggs: 2–5, white.
Food: Invertebrates.

WOODPECKERS, CUCKOOS AND BEE-EATERS

These birds all hunt invertebrates but they have evolved very different techniques for this purpose. While bee-eaters often target flying insects, woodpeckers prefer to hunt those that hide out of sight, using their bills to expose and then capture them. Cuckoos, on the other hand, have no specialized feeding strategy but eat whatever they are able to catch, locating their prey by keen observation.

Oriental cuckoo

Himalayan cuckoo *Cuculus saturatus*

Distribution: Migratory races breed in northern parts of eastern Russia, Japan and the Himalayan region, before moving to South-east Asia in the winter. Resident populations are found on the Greater Sundas.
Size: 26cm (10.5in).
Habitat: Forest.
Nest: Those of other birds.
Eggs: 1 per nest, the colour of the egg corresponds to those of the foster species.
Food: Invertebrates.

Resident and migratory populations of these birds appear not to mix very much, with the migratory cuckoos often encountered at lower altitudes. It is actually said to be possible to distinguish between the non-migratory and migratory types of this cuckoo by their calls: the former will repeatedly utter a four- rather than three-note call. During the breeding season, the cuckoo utters its call more frequently so that it is easier to locate in the forest canopy. In northern parts of their range, these cuckoos inhabit coniferous forests. In Asia, nests of the chestnut-crowned warbler (*Seicercus castaniceps*) are often parasitized by the oriental cuckoo.

Left: These cuckoos fly long distances and overwinter widely through Indonesia.

Identification: Has grey head and wings. Grey barring on white underparts, with a bare area of bright yellow skin around the eyes. Hens tend to be indistinguishable, but occasionally they are predominantly brownish with black barring in place of the grey areas. These are sometimes described as hepatic (liver-coloured) females and are a very rare sight.

Speckled piculet

Picumnus innominatus

These tiny woodpeckers are similar in habits to their larger relatives, using their bills to probe stems and branches for food. They are also sufficiently nimble in flight to feed on the wing, and can swoop down on spiders moving across bark. Speckled piculets are often observed foraging for food in the company of other birds, including various flycatchers and babblers, fire-tufted barbets and drongos. It is thought that the movements of these other birds help to stir up invertebrates, so making them easier for the piculets to catch. The nesting chamber excavated by speckled piculets is very small, measuring just 15cm (6in) in height and 6cm (2.5in) in width and depth. They often prefer to nest in rotten timber as this is easier to bore into with their bills. When breeding, these small piculets are most likely to be located by their persistent tapping rather than actually seen.

Distribution: From northern Pakistan and India east to southern China and down across the Malay Peninsula to Sumatra and Borneo. An isolated population exists in India's Western Ghats region.
Size: 10cm (4in).
Habitat: Trees, shrubs and stands of bamboo.
Nest: Hole excavated in bamboo or tree.
Eggs: 2–4, white.
Food: Insect larvae, spiders and other invertebrates.

Identification: Olive back, with a short tail. Has characteristic black and white spotted underparts. Black plumage runs through the eyes and is bordered by white streaks top and bottom. Cocks can be easily distinguished from hens by the orange patch on their forehead.

Brush cuckoo (*Cacomantis variolosus*): 24cm (9.5in)
Widely-distributed across Thailand and the Malay Peninsula, across the Sundas, south to Australia and east to the Philippines and the Solomon Islands. Head and upperparts are brownish-grey. Rufous underparts, with greyish tone to throat and upper breast. Yellow eye ring. Sexes alike.

Chestnut-winged cuckoo (*Clamator coromandus*): 45cm (18in)
Distribution extends from east India to southern China and across South-east Asia to the Greater Sundas, Sulawesi and the Philippines. Has a black head and a spectacular tufted crest. The collar is whitish and there is chestnut on the wings. The breast is a buff colour and there are grey underparts. The back and wings are blackish. Sexes are alike.

Great slaty woodpecker (*Mulleripicus pulverulentus*): 50cm (20in)
Extensive distribution from northern central parts of India through Nepal east to south-west China. Also occurs in Vietnam, Thailand and Malaysia. Present in western Indonesia east to Borneo and Palawan. Slaty-grey underparts. Paler edging to the feathers, forming white spots on the neck. Red flashes below the eyes only apparent in cock birds. Buff plumage on the throat.

Bamboo woodpecker (*Gecinulus viridis*): 28cm (11in)
Extends from Myanmar (Burma) eastwards to parts of Thailand, northern Laos and Malaysia. Cocks are predominantly greenish with a large crimson area on the head. The rump is also red. Bill greyish. Hens lack the red area on the head.

Greater yellow-naped woodpecker

Picus flavinucha

During the breeding season, the distinctive crest of these woodpeckers is used as part of their display. The sound of drumming can be heard at this time as the cock bird taps quickly and repeatedly on the side of a tree to attract a mate. Both parents help to construct a breeding chamber, which is located 2–6m (6.5–20ft) off the ground. Both also actively incubate the eggs and feed the chicks. After fledging, the young will call loudly and repeatedly if they become separated from the family group. It is quite common to encounter these woodpeckers foraging in small parties. These birds find food largely by probing in rotting vegetation rather than excavating holes in the bark. They rarely descend to ground level.

Distribution: From the Himalayan region of north-west India through Nepal to Myanmar (Burma) across South-east Asia to China. Also isolated distribution through the Malay Peninsula to Sumatra.
Size: 34cm (13in).
Habitat: Forested foothills and mountain slopes.
Nest: Rotten tree.
Eggs: 3–4, white.
Food: Wide range of invertebrates and even frogs.

Identification:
Predominantly green body, with a black tail and brown and black barring on the flight feathers. Distinctive yellow crest at the back of the head. Yellowish plumage on the throat with white spots beneath. Hens have more streaking on the throat.

Red-bearded bee-eater

Nyctyornis amictus

These bee-eaters are more likely to be seen in the middle and upper parts of the forest canopy, rather than in the darker undergrowth. Here they catch a wide variety of invertebrates in flight, preying not just on bees but also beetles, wasps and ants. They rest quietly on a chosen branch, waiting for their quarry to come within range, then fly fast and with great agility to capture it. Trees adjacent to clearings are often favoured, as these breaks in the forest provide an open area to capture prey. When breeding, the bee-eaters excavate tunnels, which can extend back 1.2m (4ft) into cliff faces and similar localities.

Identification: Pink plumage extends from in front of the eyes up over the crown. A red area beneath the bill leads down on to the chest. Yellow underside to the tail with black tips. The remainder of the body is green. The bill is dark and curves downwards at its tip. Hens have less pink plumage on the head.

Distribution: Through the Malay peninsula, apart from the southern tip, to Sumatra and Borneo.
Size: 30cm (12in).
Habitat: Lowland forested areas.
Nest: Hole in a vertical bank.
Eggs: 3–5, white.
Food: Invertebrates, including bees.

HONEYGUIDES, HORNBILLS AND BARBETS

The hornbills include some of the most magnificent birds found in the forests of Asia, not so much for their bright coloration but rather for their spectacular size and incredible bills. Barbets may be smaller, but they too have stocky bills, which in this case are used to bore into rotten wood, although they are not as talented in this respect as woodpeckers.

Malaysian honeyguide

Indicator archipelagicus

The Malaysian honeyguide is an Asian representative of a family whose members are more commonly distributed in Africa. Honeyguides have a zygodactyl perching grip, which means that their toes are arranged in a 2:2 perching configuration. They are hard to spot in the canopy, thanks both to their dull coloration and small size, and are normally solitary by nature, so very little has been documented about their habits. They do have a distinctive call, however, that consists of two notes: the first resembles the miaowing of a cat, and this is closely followed by a rattling noise. Honeyguides feed on bees as they emerge from their nests. This helps people pinpoint the nests of wild bees and find honey, which is how these birds acquired their name.

Identification: Dark olive-brown upperparts, with red irises and grey bill. Underparts greyish-white, becoming increasingly white on the lower underparts, with dark blackish streaking on the flanks. Hens lack the narrow yellow shoulder patch.

Below: The honeyguide feeds on bees, snatched from the air as they emerge from their nests.

Distribution: Ranges over the Malay Peninsula south to Sumatra and Borneo.
Size: 18cm (7in).
Habitat: Forested areas, typically in the lowlands up to an altitude of 1,000m (3,300ft).
Nest: Tree holes.
Eggs: Presently unrecorded.
Food: Bees and wasps.

Rhinoceros hornbill

Buceros rhinoceros

Distribution: In South-east Asia south through the Malay peninsula to Sumatra, Java and Borneo.
Size: 110 cm (43in).
Habitat: Lowland and hill forests.
Nest: Tree hollow.
Eggs: 2, white.
Food: Fruit and smaller vertebrates.

Right: The distinctive, long bill of this hornbill helps them to pluck fruit from otherwise inaccessible places.

The upturned casque on the top of the bill of these hornbills resembles the horn of a rhinoceros, which is, of course, why they got their name. They are most likely to be seen close by fruiting figs, which are one of their favourite foods. Deforestation of the areas inhabited by these large birds is a serious threat to their future, especially as they do not live at high densities. Individual pairs will roam over wide areas and depend on large trees for nesting purposes. As with related species, the male rhinoceros hornbill incarcerates his mate in the nest chamber, sealing the entrance with mud. He returns here regularly to feed her and their brood until the family are ready to break out of the chamber. This barrier is believed to guard against would-be predators, such as snakes.

Identification: Has a black head, breast, back and wings with a white abdomen. The tail is also white, but with a broad black band. Bill is yellowish, redder at the base with a distinctive horn-like casque above. Cock birds have a red iris, but this can range from whitish to blue in hens. Otherwise, sexes are alike.

Bushy-crested hornbill (*Anorrhinus galeritus*): 70cm (28in)
Ranges from the Malay Peninsula to Sumatra, Borneo and north Natuna. Predominantly black in colour with a loose crest at the back of the head. Has a greyish-brown tail with a black band at the base. Blue areas of skin present on the throat and around the eye. Cock birds have red irises and black bills while hens have black irises and whitish bills.

Asian black hornbill (*Anthracoceros malayanus*): 75cm (29.5in)
Found across the Malay Peninsula south to islands, including Sumatra and Borneo. Body is entirely black apart from white edging to the tail feathers. The bill and casque are whitish and the iris is red. Hens have greyish bills and pinkish skin surrounding the eyes.

Wreathed hornbill (*Aceros undulatus*): 100cm (39in)
Ranges from eastern India to south-west China, through South-east Asia and on across the Malay Peninsula to Sumatra, Java, Bali and Borneo. Has a cream-coloured head, with a reddish stripe extending from the nape. The back, wings and underparts are black. There is an unfeathered yellow gular pouch on the throat. Hens have black upperparts, a blue gular pouch and small casque.

Yellow-crowned barbet (*Megalaima henricii*): 21cm (8.5in)
Extends from the Malay Peninsula to Sumatra and Borneo. Mainly green, but darker on the wings. Has a prominent yellow forehead that extends back over the eyes. Blue plumage is present on the throat and at the back of the head. A black stripe passes through the eyes, and reddish spots are present on the nape and at the sides of the neck. Sexes alike.

Great hornbill
Buceros bicornis (E)

There is some variation in size through the extensive range of these hornbills. Mainland populations tend to be slightly smaller than their counterparts occurring on the islands. Great hornbills are most likely to be seen flying over the forest, as their large size and rather noisy flight means they are more obvious. They may also be spotted feeding in the canopy, jumping from branch to branch as they do so. Their loud call sounds rather like the barking of a small dog.

Right: The cock bird finds food and brings it to the nest for its young.

Distribution: Range extends from India to South-east Asia, across the Malay Peninsula to Sumatra.
Size: 125cm (49in).
Habitat: Forested areas.
Nest: Tree hollow.
Eggs: 2, white.
Food: Fruit and small vertebrates.

Identification: A black band encircles the face and base of the lower bill, with a cream area behind that runs down on to the upper breast. Wings predominantly black, with a white band across. White also apparent across the tips of the flight feathers when the wing is closed. Lower underparts white, as is the tail apart from a broad black band relatively close to the rounded tip. Bill yellowish, with flat-topped casque above. Cocks have red irises while hens have cream-coloured irises. Sexes are otherwise alike.

Fire-tufted barbet
Psilopogon pyrolophus

The relatively long tail and short bill of these barbets sets them apart from other species occurring in Asia. They are noisy and active by nature, often hopping from one branch to another, and occurring in small groups where food is plentiful. If danger threatens, however, fire-tufted barbets are likely to freeze, which makes them hard to observe. When roosting, they often perch with their long tails held in a vertical position. This stance allows them to roost and breed in quite small nesting chambers, which they excavate using their powerful bills.

Identification: Predominantly green, although darker on the wings and lighter on the underparts. Has a black collar around the chest with an area of yellow plumage above. Areas of black, grey and green plumage are also present on the head, with brown extending down the back of the head. Has prominent forward-pointing bristles with reddish tips evident above the upper bill. The beak itself is greenish-yellow, with two black spots on each side. Sexes alike.

Distribution: Confined to the Malay Peninsula and to parts of Sumatra.
Size: 26cm (10.5in).
Habitat: Forested areas up to 1,500m (4,900ft).
Nest: Tree holes.
Eggs: Presently unrecorded.
Food: Fruit and invertebrates.

PITTAS AND TROGONS

These brightly coloured woodland birds are surprisingly hard to spot in their natural habitat, not just because they are often shy, but also because they merge into the background thanks to the various shades and markings on their bodies. Pittas spend much of their time on or near the forest floor, while trogons tend to occupy the lower reaches, too, with the shafts of light helping to obscure their presence.

Giant pitta

Great blue pitta *Pitta caerulea*

The large, powerful bill of the giant pitta is used to feed mainly on snails, which are broken on particular stones in the pitta's territory. Cock birds maintain and defend their own areas vigorously. Earthworms are also a favoured food and occasionally they catch small snakes. These birds turn over leaf litter on the forest floor where they feed, seeking edible items. They build their nest quite close to the forest floor, usually in the fork of a suitable tree. Pairs tend to stay together throughout the year, but they can be hard to observe, as they hop away through the undergrowth at the slightest hint of danger.

Identification: A distinctive blue back, wings and tail, with pale buff underparts. The head has a blackish stripe down the centre, another stripe extending back from the eyes, and a black collar around the back of the neck. The rest of the facial plumage is a greyish colour with some black edging. Hens have a blue tail but the remainder of the plumage on the back is a chestnut brown rather than blue. Their head is brownish rather than grey.

Distribution: Extends from Myanmar (Burma) and Thailand through the Malay Peninsula to Sumatra and Borneo.
Size: 30cm (12in).
Habitat: Lowland and hill forests.
Nest: Dome-shaped, with entrance at the front.
Eggs: 2, whitish with brown speckling.
Food: Mainly invertebrates, and some small vertebrates.

Hooded pitta

Green-breasted pitta *Pitta sordida*

There are approximately a dozen recognized subspecies of hooded pitta, resulting in a considerable variation in appearance through these birds' wide range. Hooded pittas tend to be solitary by nature, seeking out food on the ground, although they will sometimes perch at least 7m (23ft) off the ground. Both members of the pair are involved in nest-building, and use a variety of vegetation to create a dome shape. The nest is well concealed on the ground, with access to the interior via a side-opening. In some parts of their range, hooded pittas are migratory by nature, and can travel long distances, often flying at night. At the onset of the rainy season they will call after dark.

Identification: Generally has a black head, with green wings and a whitish blue flash on each wing. There is a variable crimson area around the vent, which travels up to the centre of the abdomen. An area of black plumage may appear on the front. White wing patches are sometimes evident. Sexes are alike.

Distribution: Sporadic distribution from the foothills of the Himalayas through the Malay Peninsula to Indonesia, New Guinea, the Philippines and other islands in the region.
Size: 30cm (12in).
Habitat: Forested areas.
Nest: Dome-shaped mass of vegetation.
Eggs: 3–5, white with darker, often brownish spots and markings.
Food: Invertebrates.

Blue-winged pitta (*Pitta moluccensis*): 20cm (8in)
Migratory in northern parts of its range, with these birds over-wintering in more southerly localities. Occurs in China, Myanmar (Burma), Vietnam, Laos, Cambodia, Thailand and then south through the Malay Peninsula to Sumatra, Borneo and neighbouring islands, occuring at lower altitudes. Has a black crown and black stripe running through the eye that are separated by a brown band. White throat. Green on the back and wings. The underparts are buff but become crimson around the vent. Has violet-blue wing coverts and rump, with a white area present here. Very short tail. Sexes alike.

Banded pitta (*Pitta guajana*): 24cm (9.5in)
Found in Thailand and the Malay Peninsula south to Java, Sumatra and Borneo, but does not apparently appear in Singapore. Has a yellow to orange stripe above the eyes, with black plumage below, running across the sides of the face. Some white on the throat. Upperparts are chestnut-brown and the tail is a rich shade of blue. The underparts are barred in hens but violet-blue in most cock birds. The pitta's appearance is exceedingly variable, to the extent that some taxonomists believe that this species should be split into two separate species.

Red-naped trogon (*Harpactes kasumba*): 33cm (13in)
Ranges from the Malay Peninsula down to Sumatra and Borneo. Black head, with a white collar across the chest and red plumage beneath. There is also a red collar around the nape of the neck. The bill and bare skin around the eyes are bluish. The underside of the long tail is whitish. The back is brown. Hens are much paler, with a greyish head, and buff collar and underparts.

Orange-breasted trogon (*Harpactes oreskios*): 25cm (10in)
Ranges from southern China and across South-east Asia down to Sumatra, Java and Borneo. Has an olive head, brown back and tail, The underparts are orange with yellow around the vent. The wings are black and there is some white barring. Hens have grey heads and breast, with yellowish-brown underparts. The barring on their wings is black.

Garnet pitta

Red-headed scarlet pitta *Pitta granatina*

These stunningly beautiful birds tend to be well concealed in their forest habitat, where their presence is likely to be revealed initially by their song. This sounds like a whistle that becomes louder and then stops suddenly. It can carry over quite a distance. Having once located the presence of a garnet pitta, it is usually possible to get quite close without scaring the bird away, as they are not really very shy. They often disappear from tracks in the forest, preferring instead to hunt for food in the undergrowth.

Distribution: From Thailand through the Malay Peninsula to northern parts of Sumatra and Borneo.
Size: 15cm (6in).
Habitat: Lowland forests.
Nest: Domed cup of vegetation.
Eggs: 2, glossy-white with reddish-brown spots.
Food: Mainly invertebrates.

Identification: Some regional variation in the markings, with more black on the head of the Bornean race. In common, they have a fiery red area of plumage on the head, the rest of which is black apart from a pale bluish streak on the side of the head. This separates the two colours. Purplish chest and back, with rich crimson underparts. Lighter blue area on the wings. Sexes alike.

Red-headed trogon

Harpactes erythrocephalus

These trogons tend to occupy the lower levels of the thick forest in which they live. They hunt a variety of invertebrates, using a suitable perch as a watchout point before swooping down on their quarry. Like other trogons, these have the 2:2 zygodactyl perching grip, where two toes are directed forwards and two provide support behind the perch. When breeding, these birds seek out tree hollows, which may be natural spaces or created by other birds such as woodpeckers.

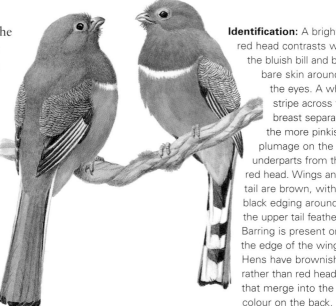

Identification: A bright red head contrasts with the bluish bill and blue, bare skin around the eyes. A white stripe across the breast separates the more pinkish plumage on the underparts from the red head. Wings and tail are brown, with black edging around the upper tail feathers. Barring is present on the edge of the wings. Hens have brownish rather than red heads, that merge into the colour on the back.

Distribution: Ranges widely from the Himalayas across Asia to southern China and south via the Malay Peninsula to Sumatra.
Size: 30cm (12in).
Habitat: Hill forest.
Nest: Tree holes.
Eggs: 2–3, buff.
Food: Invertebrates.

PHEASANTS AND SIMILAR BIRDS

This group of forest-dwelling birds are all likely to be encountered on or certainly near ground level. Some, such as the lyrebird and great argus, have difficulty in flying any distance because of their ornate plumage, whereas the brown kiwi, like others of its kind, has lost the ability to fly. Its closest relatives are actually much larger ratites such as emus and ostriches.

Superb lyrebird

Queen Victoria's lyrebird *Menura novaehollandiae*

The lyrebird resembles a pheasant and is sometimes known, misleadingly, as the native pheasant. Lyrebirds are shy and hard to spot, but the lyrebird is a talented songbird and the cock's powerful, far-carrying and lyrical song will often reveal his presence. The hens, though, have a quieter call. These birds are most likely to be glimpsed as they scurry across roads and open ground, although they can fly. They seek food on the ground, raking over leaf litter with their powerful feet. The cock bird also uses its feet to scrape up soil to form his display mounds.

Above: The lyrebird's tail feathers are more than 60cm (2ft) in length.

Identification: Dark, brownish upperparts with a coppery hue on the wings. Underparts are greyish. Adult cock birds have a distinctive train of lacy tail plumes with two long outer feathers, known as lyrates, that measure at least 60cm (24in). The tails are made up of seven pairs of feathers, with the central pair the longest. The tail itself is usually carried horizontally. Hens have shorter, more pointed tails without the filamentous plumes.

Distribution: Found in eastern Australia, from southern Queensland to Victoria. Also introduced successfully to Tasmania.
Size: Cock 100cm (38in); hen 86cm (34in).
Habitat: Wooded terrain.
Nest: Large dome-shaped nest constructed from vegetable matter.
Eggs: 1, ranges from grey to purple-brown with dark grey markings.
Food: Invertebrates, including crustaceans.

Golden pheasant

Chrysolophus pictus

Adult cock golden pheasants are naturally polygamous, living with two or three hens, but very little else has been documented about the habits of these birds in the wild. They occur in areas where there is dense vegetative cover, and because they live on the ground, observing them in these surroundings is difficult. They feed mainly on the leaves and shoots of a variety of plants, especially bamboo, as well as eating the flowers of rhododendrons.

Identification: Golden-yellow feathering on head, lower back and rump. The underparts are vibrant scarlet, merging into chestnut. The ruff or tippet on the neck is golden with black edging to the plumage and the upper back is green. Has long, mottled tail feathers. Hens in comparison are smaller and a duller colour, being essentially brown with mottling or barring on the feathers. Their tail feathers are pointed at the tips. Young birds resemble hens but have less pronounced markings.

Distribution: Occurs naturally in central China. Introduced to a few localities elsewhere, most notably in eastern England.
Size: Cock 115cm (45in); hen 70cm (27.5in).
Habitat: Wooded areas with shrubs and bamboo.
Nest: A scrape on the ground.
Eggs: 5–12, buff.
Food: Vegetation and invertebrates.

Chestnut-breasted hill partridge (*Arborophila mandellii*): 28cm (11in)
Ranges from north-east India via Bhutan to south-eastern Tibet. Chestnut crown, paler on the sides of the face, with black speckling. A greyish streak extends back from the eyes. White band with narrow black stripe beneath lies above chestnut breast feathering. Rest of the body is greyish with chestnut speckling on the flanks. Wings browner with black scalloping. Sexes alike.

Crested wood partridge (roulroul, *Rollulus roulroul*): 26cm (10.5in)
Extends from southern Myanmar (Burma) and Thailand through the Malay Peninsula to islands including Sumatra and Borneo. Highly distinctive reddish crest, edged with white. Red skin around the eyes. The rest of the plumage is dark. Hens lack the crest, and are greenish with a greyish head and brownish wings.

Crested fireback (*Lophura ignita*): Cock 66cm (26in): hen 56cm (22in)
Ranges from South-east Asia to the islands of Borneo and Sumatra. Dark bluish crest, with lighter blue wattles around the eyes. Rump is reddish. Dark blue underparts are streaked white or orange. White or buff tail feathers, depending on subspecies. Hens are predominantly brown, even blackish, with blue facial markings. White scalloping to the feathering on the underparts.

Brown kiwi

Apteryx australis

Distribution: Confined to New Zealand and present on both North and South Island as well as Stewart Island and some smaller islands.
Size: 56cm (22in).
Habitat: Forest.
Nest: In a burrow.
Eggs: 1–2, white or greenish.
Food: Invertebrates and a little fruit.

Identification: The reddish-brown plumage with darker streaking, has a distinctive hair-like texture. Long yellowish bill with bristles at the base. Strong, powerful legs. Sexes alike, although hens are larger with a longer bill.

The kiwi has become New Zealand's national emblem. These highly unusual flightless birds are essentially nocturnal in their habits. They have sensitive nostrils at the end of their bill and locate their food by smell, which is handy in the dark. They also use their bills like levers to pull out worms found in the forest soil. Hens lay what is proportionately the largest egg in the avian world relative to body size, and the yolk is relatively bigger too. This helps to nourish the chick through what is a very long incubation period, typically lasting 12 weeks. The male carries out incubation duties. Young brown kiwis resemble the adult but are smaller.

Great argus

Argusianus argus

The magnificient train created by the tail feathers of the male great argus can be up to 1.2m (4ft) long. Unfortunately, they are shy, solitary birds by nature and, therefore, hard to observe. While hens can fly without difficulty, the enlarged flight feathers of the cock, coupled with its long train affects its ability to fly any distance at all. It is not until a young male is three years old that the elongated feathers start to develop, with their transformation occurring gradually over successive moults over the next four years. They are generally used for display purposes.

Identification: Head and neck are blue, with a short blackish crest at the back of the head. Has white spots over brown plumage on the body. Large eye-like markings called ocelli in the wings. Upper breast is rusty-red. Grey coloration on the central tail feathers. Hens are much smaller, with a paler blue head and barred markings on the short tail.

Distribution: The Malay Peninsula, but absent from the south. Also found on Sumatra and Borneo.
Size: Cock 200cm (79in); hen 76cm (30in).
Habitat: Primary and logged areas of forest.
Nest: Hollow lined with grass.
Eggs: 2, creamy white.
Food: Plant matter and ants.

Left: The final stage of the cock's display involves bowing to the hen with his magnificent tail feathers held erect.

BROADBILLS AND OTHER SMALLER WOODLAND-DWELLERS

A number of Asian birds have ornamental rackets at the tips of their tail feathers, which are attached by so-called shafts, which like the racket are a continuation of the feather and quite flexible. They tend to be used for display purposes, although other ornamentations of the plumage, such as crests and bright coloration, can be seen in many broadbills.

Green broadbill

Calyptomena viridis

Distribution: From Myanmar (Burma) and western Thailand to the Malay Peninsula, Sumatra and Borneo.
Size: 17cm (7in).
Habitat: Lower levels of rainforest. Very rarely encountered in forests that have been logged.
Nest: Made of plant fibres.
Eggs: 1–3, whitish.
Food: Fruit.

These broadbills are so-called because of the size of their gape, or mouth-opening, rather than the size of their bill. They feed by foraging for fruit and their wide gape allows them to eat it whole. Their bill is very weak and lacks a cutting edge so they can only eat soft fruits such as members of the fig family. The green broadbill helps to maintain structure and diversity within the rainforest, since their feeding habits mean that they help to distribute the indigestible seeds of such plants via their droppings as they move around the forest. Their nest is an elaborate construction, resembling a bottle gourd in shape. It is suspended from a very thin branch as this helps to protect the birds from possible predators.

Identification: Has dark green plumage with three black bars across the top of the wings. A black circular area lies behind each eye. The very short tail emphasizes the outline of the plump body. The crest above the bill is larger in males. Hens are green all over but it is a lighter shade than the cocks.

Lesser cuckoo shrike

Coracina fimbriata

Despite their name, these birds are related to neither cuckoos nor shrikes, but are actually a relative of the crow family, according to DNA studies. They are so-called because they resemble the cuckoos in shape and appearance, and yet are equipped with a strong, hooked bill like shrikes, which is used for seizing invertebrates. Lesser cuckoo shrikes are birds of the forest canopy. They even nest in the canopy and are most unlikely to be seen on the ground. These cuckoo shrike's young have very different colouring, with barring evident over what is primarily white plumage. These birds have relatively harsh calls which are most likely to be uttered when they are in a group, although individuals have been known to sing on occasion.

Identification: Mainly grey, although the sides of the face, wings and tail are blackish. There is white edging to the tips of the tail feathers. The eyes are dark brown. Hens are paler and have pale grey, rather than black, feathering on their face, plus some distinctive barring on underparts.

Distribution: Ranges across the Malay Peninsula to Java and Sumatra in the Greater Sunda islands. Also Borneo.
Size: 20cm (8in).
Habitat: Lowland and hill forest.
Nest: Cup-shaped, made of vegetation.
Eggs: 3 olive-green, with brown markings.
Food: Invertebrates.

Orange-bellied leafbird

Hardwick's fruitsucker *Chloropsis hardwickii*

The relatively long bills of these birds are used to search for invertebrates among the leaves, and to probe flowers in search of nectar. The eponymous coloration of the orange-bellied leafbird allows it to blend effectively into a background of vegetation. Young, recently fledged birds are entirely green. Their nests are well hidden in forks of trees. These leafbirds are solitary by nature, although they are more likely to be seen in pairs during the breeding season. They have quite loud, meliforous calls, with cocks singing more frequently during the breeding period. Leafbirds are also talented mimics and can master the song of other birds.

Identification: Mainly green upperparts with a black mask that extends from the cheeks down on to the chest. This is broken by a blue streak that runs down below the bill. Underparts are orange-yellow. There is some dark blue plumage in the wings. The tail is dark blue. Hens are essentially green with matching underparts but have lighter blue streaks on the sides of the long bill.

Distribution: Extends from the Himalayan region to southern China and south to areas of South-east Asia down to the Malay Peninsula.
Size: 20cm (8in).
Habitat: Hill forests.
Nest: Loose cup.
Eggs: 2–3, buff-cream with pale red markings.
Food: Mainly invertebrates. Also nectar and fruit.

Greater racket-tailed drongo

Dicrurus paradiseus

Distribution: Ranges from India eastwards through South-east Asia to China and down across the Malay Peninsula to the Greater Sundas. Is present on Sumatra, Java and Bali as well as Borneo.
Size: 36cm (14in).
Habitat: Lowland forest.
Nest: Cup-shaped, made from vegetation.
Eggs: 3–4, creamy-white with dark markings.
Food: Invertebrates.

Identification: Has bluish-black plumage, with a short crest above the bill. Sharply forked tail with narrow tail shafts that end in twisted enlargements known as rackets. During the moulting period, however, the rackets may be missing or simply not developed to their full extent. The sharp, pointed bill is black as are the legs and feet. Sexes are alike.

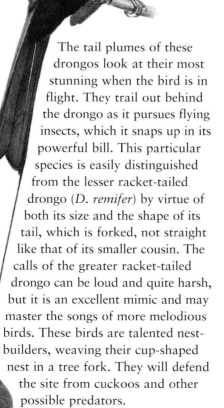

The tail plumes of these drongos look at their most stunning when the bird is in flight. They trail out behind the drongo as it pursues flying insects, which it snaps up in its powerful bill. This particular species is easily distinguished from the lesser racket-tailed drongo (*D. remifer*) by virtue of both its size and the shape of its tail, which is forked, not straight like that of its smaller cousin. The calls of the greater racket-tailed drongo can be loud and quite harsh, but it is an excellent mimic and may master the songs of more melodious birds. These birds are talented nest-builders, weaving their cup-shaped nest in a tree fork. They will defend the site from cuckoos and other possible predators.

Long-tailed broadbill (*Psarisomus dalhousiae*): 25cm (10in)
Sporadic distribution where suitable habitat is found from the eastern Himalayas across much of South-east Asia to Sumatra and Borneo. Black plumage on the top and rear of the head, with small blue and yellow areas. White collar around the neck. Greenish underparts and dark green over the back. Some blue on the wings. Blue tail. Hens may have faint yellow area on the nape.

Banded broadbill (purple-headed broadbill, *Eurylaimus javanicus*): 23cm (9in)
From Indo-China and Malaysia to Java, Sumatra and Borneo. Purple-maroon plumage on the head and underparts. Has an obvious black breast band that is absent in hens. Yellow markings on the back and wings, which are otherwise dark in colour. Bill pale blue and yellower at the tip.

Dusky broadbill (*Corydon sumatranus*): 25cm (10in)
Ranges from Indo-China down across the Malay Peninsula to Sumatra and Borneo. Pinkish-purple bill and bare skin around the eyes. The plumage is paler on the throat and blackish-brown else-where. Sexes alike.

Large wood shrike (hook-billed woodshrike, *Tephrodornis gularis*): 22cm (8.5in)
Found in western India, and from the Himalayas across South-east Asia to southern China and south through the Malay Peninsula to Java, Sumatra and Borneo. Eleven races recognized: larger birds with browner back in northern areas; smaller greyer populations in the south. Black stripe running through the eye. Rump whitish, as is the area under the throat. Underparts pale grey. Hens similar to cocks, but with browner tails.

PIGEONS AND DOVES

The diversity that exists within this group of birds can be seen at its greatest in the Australasian region, which is home to some of the most bizarre and distinctive members of this widely distributed family of birds. Vivid red, yellow and blue hues are apparent in the plumage of a number of species from the area, especially in the case of the fruit doves forming the genus Ptilinopus.

Nicobar pigeon

Caloenas nicobarica

These highly distinctive pigeons are found on many islands, particularly those least affected by human habitation. They are largely terrestrial, although if disturbed on the ground, they fly up noisily to branches close to the forest canopy. Here, their dark coloration makes them hard to spot. Nicobar pigeons have a particularly thick-walled gizzard, which allows them to grind up and digest large, heavily coated seeds without difficulty. Inevitable food shortages on small islands mean that these pigeons are often forced to forage further afield, crossing the sea to nearby larger islands, particularly during the breeding season when they are feeding their chicks.

Identification: Predominantly dark slaty-grey with green and coppery iridescent tones evident over the wings. Trail of long, relatively narrow feathers hanging down from the neck. White tail feathers and prominent swelling, known as a caruncle, on the top of the bill. Sexes alike.

Distribution: Found on islands in the Bay of Bengal eastwards as far as Palau and the Solomons. Larger numbers on breeding islands.
Size: 34cm (13in).
Habitat: Coastal forest areas.
Nest: Loose platform of twigs in a tree or bush.
Eggs: 1, white.
Food: Mainly seeds and fruit, some invertebrates.

Victoria crowned pigeon

White-tipped crown pigeon *Goura victoria*

Distribution: Northern New Guinea. Extends from Geelvink Bay to Collingwood Bay. Also found on a few smaller offshore islands here, such as Biak, Salawati and Seram.
Size: 74cm (29in).
Habitat: Lowland forest areas where the pigeons spend much of their time on the ground.
Nest: Platform of sticks, palm leaves and other vegetation.
Eggs: 1, white.
Food: Fruits, seeds and invertebrates.

This is one of three species of crowned pigeon occurring in New Guinea. These birds are likely to be encountered wandering in groups of up to ten individuals through forested areas, although in recent years they have become much scarcer near settlements as the result of being heavily hunted. If disturbed, crowned pigeons will fly up on to branches. Pairs also nest off the ground. The young bird is much smaller than its parents on fledging. It grows slowly, and will not be fully independent until more than three months old.

Identification: Has unique white tips to the blue lacy fan-like crest on the head. Remainder of the body primarily pale bluish grey, with a maroon breast and bluish underparts. Area of maroon also on the lower edges of the wing, with pale blue wing bar above. Lighter blue tip to the tail. Black feathering extends over the red irises. Sexes alike. Some individuals will display more black areas in their plumage than others.

Pied imperial pigeon (*Ducula bicolor*): 38cm (15in)
Found on islands across southern Asia down to Australia. Frequently in coastal areas; scarce in the Lesser Sundas. Creamy white with black flight feathers and broad blackish area on the tail. Dark-greyish bill and eyes. Some races have black barring on the undertail coverts. Sexes alike.

Wedge-tailed green pigeon (*Treron sphenura*): 33cm (13in)
Ranges from Himalayan region to southern China, across the Malay Peninsula to Sumatra, Java and Lombok. Greenish, with claret areas on the wings adjoining the shoulders. Pale blue wash and slight orangish hue on the breast, depending on race. Dark green barring on yellow undertail coverts. Long, wedge-shaped tail. Hens are greener.

Jambu fruit dove (*Ptilinopus jambu*): 24cm (9.5in)
Ranges from southern peninsular Thailand to Sumatra, western Java and Borneo. Red mask on the face, with a paler breast and white plumage on the lower underparts. Back of the head, wings and tail are green. Undertail coverts are brown. Hens are dark green overall, with a dull purple area on the face and greyish tone to the breast.

Barred cuckoo dove (bar-tailed cuckoo dove, *Macropygia unchall*): 37cm (14.5in)
Extends from Himalayan region to China, parts of South-east Asia and the Malay Peninsula. On to Java, Sumatra, Bali, Flores and Lombok. Greyish-pink on the head and neck, greenish suffusion on the neck. Black, with chestnut markings on the back, wings and long tail. Barring on the chest. Hens have black and chestnut underparts.

Wompoo fruit dove

Ptilinopus magnificus

Distribution: Present throughout New Guinea, except the central mountainous region. Also extends down the eastern side of Australia.
Size: Races vary widely, from 29 to 48cm (11.5 to 19in).
Habitat: Mainly evergreen rainforest.
Nest: Loose platform constructed off the ground.
Eggs: 1, white.
Food: Fruit.

Identification: Pale greyish head, with red eyes and a red bill with a yellow tip. Back, wings and tail are dark green, with a contrasting yellow wing bar. Claret breast, with the lower part of the body and under-wing feathering bright yellow. Greyish undertail coverts are edged with yellow. Underside of the flight feathers and tail are greyish. Sexes alike.

Wompoo fruit doves are so called because of the sound of their distinctive calls. Living in rainforest areas means that there will be sources of fruit available to these birds throughout the year, and they have been documented as feeding on more than 50 different types. Indigestible seeds pass through their bodies and are deposited elsewhere in the forest, and this helps to maintain their food supply in the future. Like other fruit pigeons, they have a very wide gape, enabling them to swallow fruits whole, as they are unable to bite into them with their rather weak bills. Young chicks grow very rapidly and will leave the nest at just under two weeks old.

Left: Although both sexes will share incubation duties, the cock tends to sit the longest.

Pheasant pigeon

Otidiphaps nobilis

Distribution: Much of New Guinea and various small islands.
Size: 46cm (18in).
Habitat: Hill forests.
Nest: Sticks on the ground in a tree buttress.
Eggs: 1, white.
Food: Seeds and fruit.

These unusual pigeons have no close relatives, although they actually walk a little like pheasants, with their head held forwards and their tail feathers moving rhythmically. They are seen on their own or in pairs. Being both shy and alert by nature, pheasant pigeons are very hard to observe in the field, however, unless the observer is well hidden. When displaying during the breeding period, males will swoop down from a perch, flapping their short wings to create an unusual sound that has been likened to a gunshot.

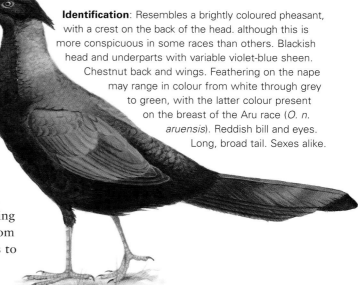

Identification: Resembles a brightly coloured pheasant, with a crest on the back of the head. although this is more conspicuous in some races than others. Blackish head and underparts with variable violet-blue sheen. Chestnut back and wings. Feathering on the nape may range in colour from white through grey to green, with the latter colour present on the breast of the Aru race (*O. n. aruensis*). Reddish bill and eyes. Long, broad tail. Sexes alike.

CORVIDS

Blackish plumage predominates in members of the crow family, although there are some spectacularly coloured members of the family found in the Australasian region, such as the vivid green hunting cissas. Corvids are an adaptable group of birds, found in a wide range of habitats, and are not easily overlooked, thanks often to their loud calls.

Forest raven

Tasmanian raven *Corvus tasmanicus*

These ravens are often seen in flocks, sometimes scavenging on rubbish tips for food. Pairs do not breed communally, preferring to seek out separate sites in tall trees, lining the inside of their nest with animal hair or wool. The colour of the eyes provides a means of aging these corvids. They are bluish grey prior to fledging and brownish by the time of fledging. It is not until they are three years old that the characteristic white coloration becomes evident.

Identification: Stocky outline with relatively short wings and tail. Glossy black coloration, with a purplish-blue, or greenish-blue, suffusion. The plumage on the abdomen tends to be held quite loosely rather than lying sleekly. Iris is whitish. Heavy, blackish bill and feet. Hens are slightly smaller.

Distribution: Tasmania and offshore islands, as well as the south-eastern corner of the Australian mainland.
Size: 52cm (21in).
Habitat: Most common in wooded areas.
Nest: Bulky cup of twigs and sticks.
Eggs: 3–6, greenish with darker markings.
Food: Carrion, invertebrates and vegetable matter.

Green magpie

Hunting cissa *Cissa chinensis*

The plumage of the green magpie can undergo an unusual but spectacular change, depending on its environmental conditions. When these birds live in relatively open country, the stronger sunlight actually bleaches their plumage. This results in the green areas becoming transformed into a light sky blue shade, while the chestnut patches change to a darker, duller shade of brown. The magpies usually occupy the lower reaches of the forest, searching in small parties through the shrubbery for invertebrates and will even eat carrion on occasions. Pairs breed on their own. The young birds have yellow bills and legs once they fledge.

Identification: Predominantly light green, with black bands running through the eyes. Broad chestnut areas cover the wings, with characteristic black and white barring where the wings meet. The undersides of the tail feathers are also black and white. Bill, legs and feet red. Sexes similar.

Distribution: Occurs over an extensive area from north-west India down to South-east Asia, and on the islands of Sumatra and Borneo.
Size: 39cm (15in).
Habitat: Edges of hill and lowland forests.
Nest: Cup-shaped platform of vegetation.
Eggs: 3–7, white through to pale green with darker markings.
Food: Invertebrates.

Slender-billed crow (*Corvus enca*):
47cm (18.5in)
Malay Peninsula and numerous offshore islands, including Sumatra, Java, Bali, Borneo, and the Sula islands. Entirely black plumage. Relatively slim bill shape. Culmen curves quite gently and is bare of feathers at its base. Sexes alike.

Large-billed crow (*Corvus macrorhynchos*):
43-59cm (17-23in)
From Himalayan region and eastern Asia to Siberia and China, through South-east Asia to the Malay Peninsula. Present on many islands, from Sumatra, Java and Borneo north to Japan and the Philippines. Entirely black but with arched and long bill. Broad wings. Hens are slightly smaller.

Brown-headed crow (*Corvus fuscicapillus*):
45cm (18in)
Found in northern New Guinea and neighbouring islands. Has a dark brown rather than blackish head and a short, square tail. The bill is large and distinctly curved. Sexes are alike, but young birds can be distinguished by their yellowish rather than black bills.

Grey crow (Bare-faced crow, *Corvus tristis*):
45cm (18in)
Widely distributed through New Guinea. Variable coloration depends partly on age. Adults blackish, with browner tone to underparts. Patches of bare skin around pale blue eyes. Hens usually smaller. Young birds are greyer overall, paler on the head and underparts than the wings.

Crested jay

Platylophus galericulatus

Distribution: From Thailand and the Malay Peninsula south to Sumatra, Java and Borneo.
Size: 33cm (13.5in).
Habitat: Lowland forest areas.
Nest: Platform of twigs.
Eggs: Presently unrecorded.
Food: Invertebrates.

Identification: Highly distinctive tail and reasonably broad crest. Adults vary from a shade bordering on black to reddish-brown, depending on the race. In all cases, a broad white area is evident on the side of the neck. Bill and legs are blackish. Sexes are alike. Juvenile birds display barred plumage on their underparts.

With their distinctive crest, these jays are instantly recognizable, but relatively little is known about their habits through their wide range. They are quite bold by nature and not instinctively given to flying away from people, especially when searching in the branches for food. They move their crest feathers up and down readily, and call quite loudly as well, uttering notes that have been likened to a rattle. The most distinctive of these races (*P. g. coronatus*) is found on Borneo and Sumatra. It is a reddish-brown overall, which is not dissimilar to the basic colour of young birds from other races.

Hooded racket-tailed treepie

Crypsirina cucullata

These particular treepies are thought to have become much rarer over recent years as a result of the deforestation of their natural habitat. These birds hunt their prey in vegetation rather than on the ground. They may sometimes be seen in small parties, but pairs will breed on their own rather than in colonies. The nest itself is often partly covered with a dome made of spiny branches, which offers increased protection against nest-raiders. Young birds can be identified for a year or so after fledging by the orange skin on the inside of their mouths. This turns yellow during their second year, and finally black. Their plumage is darker than that of an adult bird.

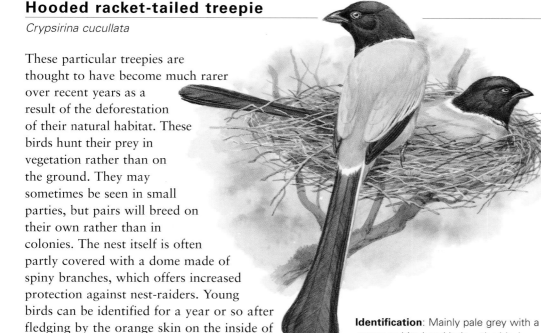

Identification: Mainly pale grey with a narrow white band below the black head. Has black wings and central tail feathers enlarged at their tips. Remainder of tail is fawn grey. Irises are dark. Sexes are alike.

Distribution: Exclusively present in Myanmar (Burma), but particularly observed in central areas.
Size: 30cm (12in).
Habitat: Lowland forest.
Nest: Cup-shaped, made from vegetation.
Eggs: 2–4, creamy to greenish white with dark markings.
Food: Invertebrates, and some berries.

BIRDS OF PARADISE AND BOWERBIRDS

The magnificent appearance of mature cock birds of these species is totally unique. There are approximately 43 distinct species of birds of paradise and 18 recognized species of bowerbird. Their distribution is centred on New Guinea, extending to neighbouring islands, south as far as Australia. Hens in contrast are much duller, as are their offspring who take several years to reach adult coloration.

Golden bowerbird

Newton's bowerbird *Prionodura newtoniana*

Cock birds are quite flamboyantly coloured, with their longer crest feathers being erected for display purposes. They are so-called because the males construct ornate structures called bowers, which are used to attract would-be mates. These bowers are carefully built from twigs and other vegetation, and well-maintained. The golden bowerbird may be the smallest of all bowerbirds, but it constructs the largest bower, up to 3m (10ft) in height. The eggs are laid in a separate site by the hen.

Identification: Cock bird has a yellow-olive head, with a short yellow crest. Wings are olive, with the underparts a rich, glistening golden shade, extending to the tail feathers. Hens have much duller coloration, with olive-brown upperparts. Underparts are greyish, with slight streaking on the throat and breast. Hens are also smaller in size.

Distribution: North-eastern Queensland, Australia
Size: 25cm (10in).
Habitat: mountain rainforest
Nest: Cup-shaped, made of vegetation.
Eggs: 2, creamy white.
Food: Fruit such as wild figs, plus insects.

Red bird of paradise

Paradisaea rubra

Hard to spot against a forest background, in spite of their striking appearance, these birds of paradise are most likely to reveal their presence by their shrill calls, which echo through the trees. Cock birds live in groups, separate from hens, and will gather at specific trees traditionally used for display purposes. Red birds of paradise tend to call down from branches in the canopy and their calls are uttered rapidly – about once every second. They forage up and down tree trunks.

Distribution: Western Papuan islands of Batanta, Waigeu and Saonek.
Size: 33cm (13in).
Habitat: Dense tropical forest.
Nest: Cup-shaped.
Eggs: 1, creamy with darker streaks.
Food: Predominantly fruit and also invertebrates.

Identification: Long, delicate red feathering on the flanks. Green plumage extends over the top of the head. Unusual curled, ribbon-like tail wires, which can be as long as 59cm (23in) when extended. Hens are less bright but have a yellow nuchal collar.

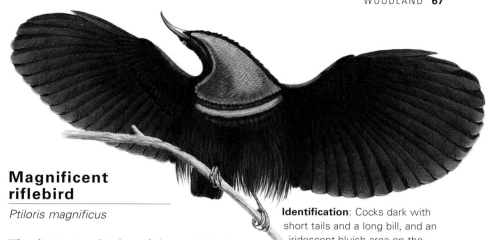

Great bowerbird (Queensland bowerbird, *Chlamydera nuchalis*): 37.5cm (15in)
Present in northern Australia from Broome in the west of the area to the coast of Queensland. The cock has grey on the underparts, mottled upperparts and a whitish edging to the brownish plumage over the wing and rump. A striking lilac crest is apparent on the nape of the neck. Hens may lack this crest feathering and are paler with less mottling.

Arfak astrapia (black astrapia, *Astrapia nigra*): 76cm (30in)
Restricted to the Arfak mountains of Vogelkop, north-western New Guinea. Cock has a broad purplish tail, bluish-green coloration on the throat and a blackish chest area with a copper-coloured surround. Head and wings dark, with back and underparts being green. Hens are greyish-brown, with barring on their tail and underparts.

King bird of paradise (*Cicinnurus regius*): 15cm (6in)
New Guinea and nearby islands. Cock bird has red upperparts and white underparts. Very short tail, with two wires terminating in green discs. Bill yellowish. Both sexes have blue legs. Hens are mainly brownish-greyish, with barred underparts.

Wilson's bird of paradise (*Cicinnurus respublica*): 17cm (7in)
Solely confined to the Western Papuan islands of Waigeo and Batanta. Cock birds have a blue cap on the head, yellow mantle, red back and wings. The underparts are green. The short tail is black and the tail wires spiral. Hens also have a blue cap and a black area over the rest of the head, but the wings and back are greyish brown, and the underparts are heavily barred.

Magnificent riflebird

Ptiloris magnificus

The distinctive display of the cock bird involves puffing out its chest feathering and stretching out its wings. Tall trees, often covered in vines and other creepers, are favoured as display sites. The sudden explosive calls of cock birds resemble the sound of a rifle firing, although distinctive regional dialects exist in the two separate New Guinea populations. The magnificent riflebirds found in the east – in Sepik, for example – make a more guttural noise than the westerly populations. These birds are sometimes seen foraging on trees in the company of babblers and pitohuis, seeking out invertebrates that have been disturbed by their companions.

Identification: Cocks dark with short tails and a long bill, and an iridescent bluish area on the crown and breast. Females also have a long elongated bill, but are basically brown in colour, with barring on their underparts.

Distribution: Parts of New Guinea and Queensland, Australia.
Size: 37cm (14.5in).
Habitat: Forested, usually upland areas.
Nest: Deep cup-shaped nest, often built in a palm.
Eggs: 2, creamy with some darker markings.
Food: Fruit and invertebrates.

Black-billed sicklebill

Buff-tailed sicklebill *Drepanornis albertisii*

Distribution: North-west, central and east New Guinea.
Size: 35cm (14in).
Habitat: Mountain forests.
Nest: Broad cup-shape.
Eggs: 1, pinky cream with red and grey blotching.
Food: Fruit and invertebrates.

It is thought that the long, narrow curved bill of these birds probably helps them to feed. Although not rare, very little is known about the black-billed sicklebill's habits and this is partly because they usually occur in the upper branches of the tallest trees, making them hard to observe. In addition, their coloration enables them to blend into their surroundings very effectively. It is thought that they feed in a woodpecker-like fashion on tree bark, using their long bills to probe for invertebrates that might be lurking in holes in the trunk or under loose bark. Their distribution does not appear to be consistent throughout their range, even in areas of apparently identical habitat. On occasions, the powerful musical call of a cock bird may be heard.

Identification: The stunning beauty of the cock bird is most apparent during the display, when the tufted areas of feathering on the sides of the body are held erect. Hens lack these fan tufts, are brownish with mottled plumage on the underparts, and also have longer, more pointed tail feathers, darker in colour than those of the cocks.

CASSOWARIES AND PARROTS

These groups include not just one of the largest birds of the world, in the guise of the double-wattled cassowary, but also a representative of the group of smallest parrots in the world, which are appropriately known as pygmy parrots. They represent two extremes within the avian order that can be encountered within the forest environment in the Australasian region.

Double-wattled cassowary

Casuarius casuarius

Distribution: New Guinea, apart from northern-central region and the central highlands. Also on the Aru Islands. Two separate Australian populations found in north-eastern Queensland.
Size: 130–170cm (51–67in).
Habitat: Rainforest areas.
Nest: Depression on the ground.
Eggs: 3–5, pale to dark green.
Food: Mainly fruit, some animal matter.

These gigantic birds of the forest are quite able to kill a person if cornered, disembowelling them with a blow from the long inner claw present on their feet. The colour of the bare skin on the cassowary's head and neck changes with mood, becoming more brightly coloured when the bird is excited or angry. Hens mate with a number of different cock birds, leaving the male to hatch and rear the chicks on their own. The young cassowaries stay with the male for up to nine months.

Identification: Massive, predominantly black flightless bird with immensely powerful feet. Has a large blade-like casque on the head and a powerful bill. Head tends to be bluish overall with two striking reddish wattles hanging down the neck. Hens have a larger casque and are also much heavier, weighing up to 58kg (128lb), whereas males rarely exceed 34kg (75lb).

Red-breasted pygmy parrot

Mountain pygmy parrot *Micropsitta bruijnii*

As their name suggests, the pygmy parrots are the smallest of all parrots, with their distribution confined to islands off South-east Asia. This particular species is found at higher altitudes than are other pygmy parrots, and also uses trees rather than arboreal termite nests as breeding sites. They have jerky movements, rather reminiscent of nuthatches (*Sitta* species), and cling close to the bark as they search for the lichens growing on trees, which form the major part of their diet.

Identification: Has a buff-red crown, becoming bluish-purple at the back of the neck. The throat and cheeks are also buff-red and become yellowish around the bill. The remainder of the underparts are red while the back and wings are mainly dark green. Hens have a blue crown with buff orange cheeks, although these areas are a paler shade than in the cock.

Distribution: Buru, Seram and central New Guinea east to the Bismarck Archipelago and the Solomon Islands.
Size: 8cm (3in).
Habitat: Forest areas.
Nest: Tree holes.
Eggs: 3, white.
Food: Plant matter.

Edwards's fig parrot

Psittaculirostris edwardsii

These chunky parrots are very agile when feeding, being able to eat without difficulty when hanging upside down from a branch. As their name suggests, figs form an important part of their diet, and hundreds of these parrots may congregate in an area where fruit is freely available. More commonly, however, they live in pairs or small groups, and can be hard to spot in the canopy where they feed, because of their small size, even though they are not especially shy by nature.

Distribution: Restricted to north-eastern area of New Guinea.
Size: 18cm (7in).
Habitat: Lowland forest.
Nest: Tree holes.
Eggs: 2–3, white.
Food: Fruit and some invertebrates.

Identification: Cock birds have a green crown with a narrow black stripe extending behind the eye. Yellow area beneath eye, along with some sky blue feathering, while the cheeks, breast and abdomen are scarlet, broken with variable violet markings across the throat. Hens are duller in colour, with green rather than red plumage below the collar. Young birds of both sexes resemble the hen, although their ear coverts are of a more greenish-yellow shade.

Brehm's tiger parrot (*Psittacella brehmii*): 24cm (9.5in)
Three distinct populations: central highlands of New Guinea; north-east Huon Peninsula; and Vogelkop, where they live in areas of mountain forest. Cock has olive-brown head, partial yellow collar at the sides of the head, green underparts, red undertail coverts. Green feathering on the back is edged with black. Hens similar but display barring on the breast and lack any yellow plumage on the neck.

Pesquet's parrot (vulturine parrot, *Psittrichas fulgidus*): 46cm (18in)
Two distinct populations on New Guinea. One confined to the Vogelkop, the other extending through the central area towards the Huon Peninsula and the south-east. Unmistakable with bare skin on the head, predominantly black plumage with barring on the chest and brilliant scarlet red areas on the wings and underparts. Looks more like a vulture in flight than a parrot, soaring readily above the forest. Sexes alike.

Papuan king parrot (green-winged king parrot, *Alisterus chloropterus*): 38cm (15in)
Found in northern, central and south-eastern parts of New Guinea. Cocks have a red head and underparts, green wings with distinctive yellow-green barring and purple over the back, which may be darker than the wings, depending on the race. They also have a long dark tail. Hens are duller in colour, with a green head, breast and wings, except in the case of the northern race (*A. c. moszkowskii*), which resembles the cock but with a green mantle.

Timor crimson-wing parakeet (*Aprosmictus jonquillaceus*): 35cm (14in)
Ranges up to altitudes of 2,600m (8,500ft) on the Indonesian islands of Timor, Weta and Roti. Predominantly green, but with blue suffusion on the back that is absent in hens. Characteristic crimson red coloration apparent on the wing coverts. Turquoise-blue rump. Broad green tail. Bill reddish.

Eclectus parrot

Eclectus roratus

This species represents the most extreme example of sexual dimorphism among all parrots. It was thought for many years following their discovery that the cock and hen were actually two separate species. There are around ten distinct races, and it is the appearance of the hen birds that differs most markedly. The feeding habits of these parrots are such that they are often seen in agricultural areas, readily feeding on crops ranging from bananas to maize. They are dependent on mature trees as nest sites however, choosing chambers that may be up to 6m (20ft) in depth.

Identification: Thick-set, with quite short, broad tails. Mostly green, with a yellowish upper bill and a red patch on the flanks. Hens have black bills. They are bright red, typically with purplish markings on the underparts, although these markings depend on the race. You can determine a juvenile's sex in the nest, from the colour of its plumage.

Distribution: Centred on New Guinea, but extends widely, to islands to both the west and east. A small population is also present on the Cape York peninsula, Australia.
Size: 35cm (14in).
Habitat: Lowland forests, often in coastal regions. Also in mangroves.
Nest: Tree hollow.
Eggs: 2, white.
Food: Fruit, buds and seeds.

BIRDS OF PREY

Although dense stretches of woodland may not appear to represent the best hunting possibilities for birds of prey, it is remarkable how these predatory birds have adapted to this environment. This is also reflected by the way in which a number of species have become highly specialized in their hunting habits, such as the crested honey buzzard.

Blyth's hawk eagle

Spizaetus alboniger

These strong aerial hunters seize their prey in the upper levels of the forest, taking not just birds but also lizards, bats and other mammals. They are watchful hunters, like other hawk eagles, often swooping on their quarry from a favoured perch that affords good visibility of any movements in the canopy. On occasions, these eagles are mobbed by groups of smaller birds, such as drongos, seeking to drive the bigger birds away, and the resulting disturbance draws attention to the birds' presence. These hawk eagles may also be seen circling and soaring over the forest. They are quite rare through their range, occurring at low population densities.

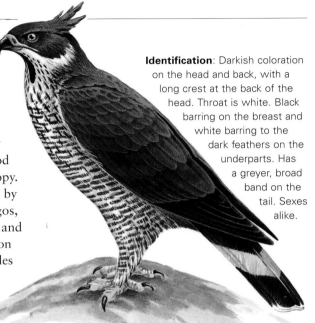

Identification: Darkish coloration on the head and back, with a long crest at the back of the head. Throat is white. Black barring on the breast and white barring to the dark feathers on the underparts. Has a greyer, broad band on the tail. Sexes alike.

Distribution: From southern Myanmar (Burma) through the Malay Peninsula to Sumatra and small nearby islands. Also present in north Borneo.
Size: 58cm (23in).
Habitat: Upland forest areas.
Nest: Bulky nest built at the top of a tree.
Eggs: 1, whitish with darker markings.
Food: Vertebrates.

New Guinea harpy eagle

Kapul eagle *Harpyopsis novaeguineae*

These forest eagles are formidable hunters, taking a wide range of prey, including tree kangaroos and wallabies and even domestic animals such as puppies. The distinctive ruff of feathers around the face helps them trace the source of sounds, and these birds also have keen eyesight. In addition to swooping down on their quarry, these eagles run and bound over the ground for short distances using their long legs. Breeding pairs return to the same site every year, choosing a tree with no lower branches and amassing a large platform of sticks near the crown at a height of 20m (66ft).

Identification: Brown upperparts with darker barring across the tail, which ends in a dark tip. The breast is brown and the underparts white. Long unfeathered legs with yellow feet. Has a crest that can be raised at the back of the head, and a pronounced ruff of feathers around the face. Hens are larger, but otherwise alike.

Right: Barred markings can be seen under the wings when the bird is in flight.

Distribution: Confined to the island of New Guinea.
Size: 90cm (35in).
Habitat: Rainforest up to 3,200m (10,500ft).
Nest: Platform of sticks.
Eggs: 1, white with darker markings.
Food: Vertebrates.

Crested serpent eagle

Spilornis cheela

There is a considerable variation in the size of these eagles through their wide range. The largest examples occur in northern India and Nepal and the smallest individuals are found further south on the Nicobar islands, off India's coast. Their name partly derives from the snakes that are a regular feature of their diet. The crested serpent eagle is likely to be observed soaring over the forest, although when hunting it usually rests on a perch, swooping down to grab snakes or lizards from either trees or the ground. Crested serpent eagles will sometimes prey on other vertebrates, including aquatic species such as eels, and have also been observed catching crabs.

Identification: Blackish brown upperparts, but has more variable underparts that range from reddish to dark brown and broken by white markings. The bill is blackish at the tip and yellow at its base. Broad greyish bar across the tail feathers. Sexes alike.

Distribution: India and Sri Lanka eastwards to China. Across South-east Asia and the Malay Peninsula south to Sumatra, Java and Borneo.
Size: 41–75cm (16–29.5in).
Habitat: Wooded areas, but not dense forest.
Nest: Small cup-shaped with grass lining.
Eggs: 1, whitish with darker markings.
Food: Primarily reptiles.

Lesser fish eagle (*Ichthyophaga humilis*): 60cm (24in)
Extends from Kashmir through the Himalayas into Myanmar (Burma) and Hainan, then south through the Malay Peninsula to Sumatra, Borneo, Sulawesi and neighbouring islands. Cock has a greyish head and neck, with brown back, wings and tail. White underparts. Greyish hooked bill and legs. Sexes are alike.

Long-tailed buzzard (*Henicopernis longicauda*): 60cm (24in)
Found on the west Papuan islands, Aru islands and New Guinea. Light and darker brown barring on the wings and tail. The head is brown with lighter chestnut ear patches. Whitish streaking around the neck and down on to the breast. The abdomen has a buff rather than whitish tone. Hens are larger.

Little eagle (*Hieraaetus morphnoides*): 55cm (22in)
Present all over New Guinea apart from the central mountainous region, and throughout Australia apart from Tasmania. These eagles occur in both a light and a dark form. The darker morphs are a deeper shade of brown, especially on the head and underparts. Lighter individuals have whitish areas on the greater wing coverts. Hens are larger.

Doria's hawk (*Megatriorchis doriae*): 69cm (27in)
Present on New Guinea and neighbouring Batanta Island. Light brown with black barring on the upperparts. Grey tail with black banding. White underparts with dark streaking, which is most pronounced on the chest. Hens are larger.

Crested honey buzzard

Pernis ptilorhynchus

The far-north Asiatic population of the crested honey buzzard winters in the far south of the species' range on the Greater Sundas. It is possible to distinguish between these birds and the resident population, however, thanks to the former's lack of a pronounced crest. The feeding habits of these buzzards are highly distinctive, since they attack the nests of wild bees and wasps, eating not just the insects and their larvae but also the honeycomb. Although crested honey buzzards prefer to raid tree nests, they are quite able to use their strong feet to dig out nests on the ground. They also prey on other social insects such as ants and termites.

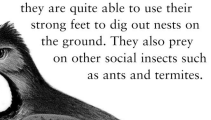

Distribution: Across India and South-east Asia, south across the Malay Peninsula to islands including Sumatra, Java and Borneo. Also a northern population, which ranges eastwards through southern Siberia.
Size: 57cm (22in).
Habitat: Wooded areas up to 1,800m (5,900ft).
Nest: Platform of twigs.
Eggs: 2, whitish with brownish markings.
Food: Wasps and bees.

Identification: Variable. Brown predominantly, which ranges from a light to darker shade depending on the individual. Broad grey band across the tail feathers. Has white markings around the neck and on the underparts. Crest may be evident on the back of the neck. The bill is grey. Legs and feet are yellow. Sexes alike.

CHATS AND OTHER INSECTIVOROUS BIRDS

All these birds, ranging from the tiny emu-wren to the pied currawong, hunt invertebrates, although they adopt very different feeding strategies. The savanna nightjar hunts on the wing and is a nocturnal hunter, whereas the fairy martin also hunts on the wing but during the hours of daylight. Others, such as the chats, prefer to look for their food on the ground.

Rufous-crowned emu-wren

Stipiturus ruficeps

Distribution: Extends from western Australia east to Queensland. Separate population in the south-east.
Size: 14.5cm (5.5in).
Habitat: Dry, treeless country.
Nest: Oval structure made from vegetation.
Eggs: 2–3, white with brownish blotching.
Food: Invertebrates, and occasionally seeds.

The habitat requirements of these birds appear to be precise as they are found in areas of spinifex and porcupine grass, especially where there are isolated shrubs. Their small size makes it difficult to track their exact distribution, particularly as they skulk in the vegetation for long periods, although they sometimes reveal their presence by high-pitched calls. If disturbed, they fly a short distance before returning to the grass. Emu-wrens get their name from their tail feathers, which are long and stiff, resembling those of emus. They are unique in having just six tail plumes, fewer than any other bird in the world.

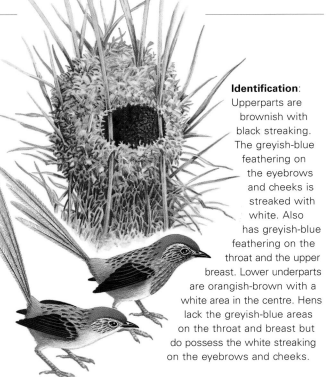

Identification: Upperparts are brownish with black streaking. The greyish-blue feathering on the eyebrows and cheeks is streaked with white. Also has greyish-blue feathering on the throat and the upper breast. Lower underparts are orangish-brown with a white area in the centre. Hens lack the greyish-blue areas on the throat and breast but do possess the white streaking on the eyebrows and cheeks.

Savanna nightjar

Allied nightjar *Caprimulgus affinis*

Nocturnal by nature as their name suggests, the persistent vocalizations of these nightjars helps to reveal their presence. They will call almost constantly for approximately half an hour, both at dusk and dawn, uttering a distinctive and repetitive cheeping sound. During the day, these nightjars rest in a relatively secure location on the ground, where their cryptic coloration helps to conceal their presence. They have also adapted well to urban living, however, and are not averse to resting out of sight on the roofs of buildings. The savanna nightjar is also drawn to hunt around electric lights, such as street lamps, as these attract night-flying invertebrates such as moths.

Identification: Short tail. Dark brown and black overall with barring on the tail and body. Has white outer tail feathers. Small bill is surrounded by bristle-like feathers. The white throat band is split into two. Hens lack the white outer tail feathers and have a more rufous-brown coloration.

Distribution: Extends eastwards from India to southern China south across South-east Asia to the Sunda islands, Sulawesi and the Philippines.
Size: 22cm (9in).
Habitat: Dry, open coastal areas.
Nest: Scrape on the ground.
Eggs: 2, buff with darker markings.
Food: Invertebrates.

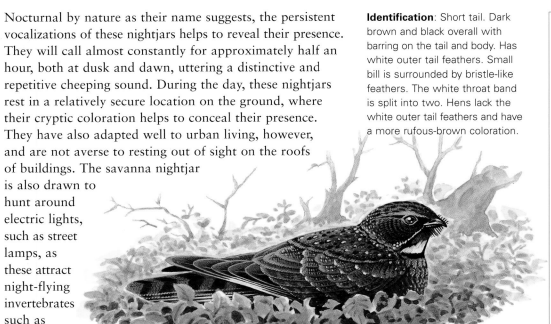

Desert chat

Gibberbird *Ashbyia lovensis*

These chats are most likely to be observed on the ground, where their upright gait helps them to run fast if necessary. When flying short distances, they flutter low across the ground but they can fly strongly too, as befits a nomadic species that moves from one area to another in search of favourable conditions. The desert chat lines a scrape on the ground with vegetation to disguise its presence. It is not uncommon to see pairs together, although they are easily overlooked as they are well concealed on the ground. Occasionally, flocks of up to 20 individuals may be spotted, and often pairs choose to nest quite close together.

Identification: Brownish-black, mottled upperparts, with white tip to the black tail. Yellowish underparts, although the rump is orangish in colour. Has a narrow and pointed black bill. Dark eyes. Hens are similar but duller in appearance. Both sexes adopt an upright pose when standing.

Distribution: Southern-central parts of Australia near border areas between New South Wales, Queensland, Northern Territory and South Australia, although the precise range is not well known.
Size: 12.5cm (5in).
Habitat: Arid areas.
Nest: Scrape on the ground.
Eggs: 3, white with reddish-brown markings.
Food: Invertebrates.

Long-tailed shrike (black-capped shrike, *Lanius schach*): 25cm (10in)
Extensive range from Iraq and India east to China, and south across the Malay Peninsula to the Greater Sundas and other islands, including the Philippines and New Guinea. Has either a black and grey or black head depending on the race. Mainly white underparts, with a rufous-brown mantle, back and flanks. Wings are black with a white area. Has a long tail and black on its upperparts. Sexes are alike.

Fairy martin (cliff swallow, *Hirundo ariel*): 12.5cm (5in)
Widely distributed across Australia apart from the south-western corner and the northern part of the Cape York peninsula. Normally absent from Tasmania. Has a pale rust-red colour to the crown and whitish underparts. Wings and tail are blackish. The rump is white. Sexes alike.

Pied currawong (pied bell-magpie, *Strepera graculina*): 49cm (19in)
Occurs down the entire eastern side of mainland Australia. Predominantly black, with a long, black, powerful bill and striking yellow eyes. There are white areas on the flight feathers, as well as at the base of the tail and in the vicinity of the vent. The tip of the tail is also white. Sexes are alike.

Pied butcherbird (black-throated butcherbird, *Cracticus nigrogularis*): 37.5cm (15in)
Occurs all over Australia apart from the south-west corner and the south-east coastal region. Black head. Black areas on the wings and tail. The rest of the body is white. The sexes are alike. Young birds have brownish rather than black coloration.

Crimson chat

Ephthianura tricolor

These smallish birds are one of Australia's most nomadic species and travel across huge distances of inhospitable territory. They survive even when invertebrates are scarce. As these form the bulk of their diet, the crimson chat feeds instead on nectar gathered from desert plants. Remarkably, these plants can produce large amounts of nectar and this encourages the chat to fertilize their flowers by transferring pollen between the blooms as they feed on them. Probably correlating with flowering times, crimson chats are sometimes seen in quite large numbers where they have not occurred before, and then disappear just as suddenly as they came.

Distribution: Across the interior of Australia from the west coast, although generally absent from other coastal areas.
Size: 12cm (5.5in).
Habitat: Shrubland and open country.
Nest: Cup-shaped, located just off the ground.
Eggs: 3–4, white with darker spots.
Food: Invertebrates and nectar.

Identification: Crimson cap. Has blackish-brown sides to the face that extend over the mantle and back, although the wing feathers have paler edges. The throat is white; the underparts are crimson. Hens are easily distinguished by the light brown colour of their crown, and the red patches on their white underparts.

AUSTRALIAN PARAKEETS

Although grass parakeets are smaller than rosellas, both have comparable habits, having evolved to feed primarily on the ground, searching out grass seeds and other similar titbits. Members of both groups occur widely through Australia. Rosellas are easily distinguished from parakeets of similar size by means of the scalloping on their back and wings.

Bourke's grass parakeet

Neophema bourkii

The relatively large eyes of these parakeets are an indication that they are most active at dusk and daybreak, resting when the sun is at its hottest, and have been known to fly after dark. They feed on the ground, moving on to new localities if a shortage of food or water threatens. Although these birds are usually encountered in small groups, much larger congregations, of up to a thousand birds, have been observed at larger waterholes in times of drought. Where conditions are favourable, they rear two rounds of chicks in succession: the first-round offspring disperse rather than stay near the nest site.

Identification: Has unusual coloration with brownish upperparts that often have a slightly rosy hue. The underparts are very pinkish, especially the abdomen. Has blue plumage on forehead, white around the eye and flecking on the face. Has violet-blue flight feathers and paler blue undertail coverts. Sexes are similar, although hens do not have the blue forehead-plumage.

Distribution: Interior of Australia, from Geraldton in Western Australia eastwards to South Australia. Separate population in south-west Queensland and the adjacent area of New South Wales.
Size: 20cm (8in).
Habitat: Scrubland and lightly wooded areas.
Nest: Tree hole.
Eggs: 3–6, white.
Food: Grass seeds and other vegetation.

Splendid grass parakeet

Scarlet-chested parakeet *Neophema splendida*

Distribution: Southern-central parts of Australia and western and south Australia.
Size: 22cm (9in).
Habitat: Semi-desert areas.
Nest: Hollow tree.
Eggs: 3–6, white.
Food: Grass seeds and other vegetation.

These nomadic parakeets move readily from the Great Victoria Desert region into neighbouring areas. These irruptions are triggered by a search for more favourable conditions. They can survive quite well without ready access to drinking water, however, as succulent plants help to meet much of their fluid requirement. They feed mainly on grass seeds and are most commonly sighted in areas of spinifex. Splendid grass parakeets have developed clever feeding techniques whereby they hold down seed heads with one foot and prise the seeds out with their bill.

Identification: Scarlet plumage on the breast and yellow lower underparts distinguishes the cock bird from all other grass parakeets. The facial area is blue, becoming paler around the eyes. Crown, neck, back and wings are green, apart from blue areas on the edge of the wing. Hens are similar but duller, with a green breast and paler blue face.

Adelaide rosella

Platycercus adelaidae

Some ornithologists believe that this bird is a naturally occurring hybrid between the crimson rosella (*P. elegans*) and the yellow rosella (*P. flaveolus*). Even so, these parakeets breed true, and it is estimated that they have a population of more than 50,000. There is certainly not a significant overlap between the distributions of the two suggested ancestral species today.

Distribution: Southern Australia, being present in the Mount Lofty and southern Flinders ranges.
Size: 36cm (14in).
Habitat: Lightly wooded areas.
Nest: Tree holes.
Eggs: 4–5, white.
Food: Mainly seeds and fruit.

Identification: Variable coloration but appearing an orange-red colour overall. Often a little lighter at the top of the wings, with the scalloped patterning here both yellow and orange, depending on the individual. Wings are mauvish in the vicinity of the flight feathers and the tail. Sexes alike. Young birds are less colourful and do not acquire adult plumage until their second year.

Turquoisine grass parakeet (*Neophema pulchella*): 20cm (8in)
Found in eastern Australia, from Queensland south via eastern New South Wales into Victoria. Blue area surrounding the black bill, extending back to the eyes. Yellowish underparts, but more orange on the breast. Crown, back, wings and tail are green, apart from the red bar and the prominent areas of blue on the wings. Hens lack the red plumage on the wings and have whitish lores, which help to distinguish them from hen scarlet-chested parakeets.

Blue-winged grass parakeet (*Neophema chrysostoma*): 20cm (8in)
Often migrates across the Bass strait to breed on Tasmania, returning to overwinter on mainland Australia and can be found as far north as Queensland. Yellow area around the bill, with a dark and light band of blue above, connecting the eyes. Olive-green upperparts and chest, with yellow abdomen. Prominent areas of dark blue on the wings. Hens are less brightly coloured.

Pale-headed rosella (mealy rosella, *Platycercus adscitus*): 30cm (12in)
Found in north-eastern Australia, from the Cape York peninsula down to northern New South Wales. Yellowish plumage on the top of the head and white on the sides. Has blue cheek marking (depending on the race) and underparts. Red undertail coverts. Yellowish-white scalloping to the black feathers on the back, with blue on the wing. Sexes are alike.

Eastern rosella

Platycercus eximius

Distribution: From south-eastern Queensland, continuing southwards along the coast into the south-eastern part of South Australia. Also found on Tasmania.
Size: 33cm (13in).
Habitat: Grassland to wooded areas.
Nest: Tree hole.
Eggs: 4–9, white.
Food: Seeds and fruit.

Rosellas form part of the 'broadtail' group of parakeets, so-called because their tail feathers do not taper to a point unlike those of many other parakeets. The eastern rosella is a highly adaptable species. Small introduced populations are now established in New Zealand, where it has successfully adapted to living in pine forests. Eastern rosellas often feed on the ground and can be seen hunting for seeds on roadside verges, especially early in the morning. They then roost quietly through the warmer hours of the day. The hen incubates the eggs alone, although the cock bird may join her in the nest.

Identification: Bright red head with white cheek patches. Has yellowish-green underparts that become green towards the vent and red undertail coverts. The scalloped edging on the back varies from yellow to green, depending on the race. The rump is green. The tail feathers become bluish at their tips. The red is slightly duller in hens and the white cheek patches are not so clearly defined.

BUDGERIGARS AND OTHER AUSTRALIAN PSITTACINES

Although the budgerigar is the best-known of all Australia's psittacines, this is a large group of birds which display a considerable diversity in appearance. In Australia, the terms 'parrot' and 'parakeet' tend to be used almost interchangeably. Elsewhere, however, the description of 'parakeet' is usually applied to psittacines with long tails.

Princess of Wales' parakeet

Queen Alexandra's parakeet *Polytelis alexandrae*

Distribution: Australian interior, from the Great Sandy Desert of Western Australia east to the Northern Territory via Alice Springs and as far as the extreme west of Queensland.
Size: 46cm (18in).
Habitat: Arid country.
Nest: Tree hollow.
Eggs: 4–6, white.
Food: Mainly seeds.

Very little is known about these enigmatic parakeets, which turn up unexpectedly in a region and then disappear again for many years. It used to be thought they were truly nomadic, but recent studies suggest the centre of their distribution is in the vicinity of Lake Tobin, from where they irrupt at intervals to other parts of their range. These parakeets are opportunistic when breeding, with pairs usually choosing to nest when food is plentiful. They seek their food on the ground.

Identification: Delicate pastel shades predominate in the plumage. Pale blue is evident on the crown and a pinkish hue on the throat. Has bright green plumage across the back and a bright blue rump. Hens lack the pale blue crown and their back is duller in tone.

Barraband parakeet

Superb parrot *Polytelis swainsonii*

There is some seasonal movement of these parakeets as they often move further north at the approach of winter. During the breeding season, small flocks of male barraband parakeets often forage for food alone. Pairs may nest in a loose colonial system of as many as six pairs, so hens are in the neighbourhood at this time. Barraband parakeets are quite opportunistic when seeking food, and they are not averse to feeding in agricultural areas, often descending into fields to pick up any seeds remaining after the harvest. These birds generally prefer feeding on the ground, although they will forage in the trees as well.

Identification: Stunning yellow face, with a red band separating it from the breast. The remainder of the plumage is bright green apart from the tip of the tail and the flight feathers which are a bluish-black. The bill is red. Hens lack the bright yellow facial colouring and instead have a blue tinge to their green facial plumage and at the bend of the wing.

Distribution: Mainly confined to the Australian state of New South Wales, but also found to the south just across the border in northern Victoria.
Size: 42cm (16.5in).
Habitat: Open woodland.
Nest: Suitable hole in a tree.
Eggs: 4–6, white.
Food: Seeds, fruit and vegetation.

Cockatiel

Nymphicus hollandicus

Distribution: Occurs over most of Australia, although generally not in coastal areas, and absent from central-southern parts. Not present on Tasmania.
Size: 30cm (12in).
Habitat: Mainly arid areas.
Nest: Tree hollow.
Eggs: 4–7, white.
Food: Seeds and fruit.

These elegant relatives of the cockatoo live in flocks and are relatively nomadic by nature. Their whistling calls are much quieter than the cockatoos', and cock birds vocalize more than hens. Large flocks, hundreds of birds in size, may be seen in agricultural areas. Cockatiels often prefer to feed on the ground, with some flock members acting as sentinels, warning of the approach of possible danger. Once alerted, the whole flock will wheel away, so it can be quite difficult to approach these cockatiels closely.

Identification: Grey overall with white areas on the wings. Crest feathers are yellow with yellow sides to the face and orange ear coverts. Dark grey tail. Hens are duller. They have a greyish-yellow colour on the head. Their tails are barred on the underside with yellow and this also occurs on the underside of the wings in flight.

Regent parakeet (rock pebbler, *Polytelis anthopeplus*): 41cm (16in)
There are two widely separated populations on Australia: one is found in the south-west of Western Australia, while the other extends east across the South Australian border. Yellowish with a green mantle and reddish area on the wing. Bluish-black flight feathers and tail. Hens are greener, with a greyer tone to their underparts.

Port Lincoln parakeet (*Barnardius zonarius*): 44cm (17in)
Ranges from western to central parts of Australia, mainly across the southern part of the continent. Has a blackish head, dark blue cheek patches and a yellow collar around the neck. The remainder of the body is mainly green, with a yellower abdomen, depending on the race. There may be a red frontal band. Hens are duller in colour.

Blue bonnet (*Northiella haematogaster*): 30cm (12in)
There are four distinct populations present in the southern half of Australia and these range from the western side of the continent to Queensland. Has a prominent dark blue area on the face. The rest of the plumage has greyish tones, apart from the abdomen which is pale yellow with reddish markings. Undertail coverts may be red, depending on race. Blue area on the sides of the wings. Hens are less blue on the face.

Budgerigar

Melopsittacus undulatus

Distribution: Ranges over most of Australia, apart from coastal areas. Not present on Tasmania.
Size: 18cm (7in).
Habitat: Arid country.
Nest: Tree holes.
Eggs: 4–8, white.
Food: Mainly grass seeds.

Wild budgerigars are much smaller, more streamlined birds than their domesticated cousins, with the garish, domestic colour variants virtually unknown in wild flocks. When flocks are harried by a bird of prey, the budgerigars fly in tight formation, making it hard for the would-be predator to target an individual unless there is a straggler. Budgerigars are vulnerable to water shortages and so in times of drought, their numbers may plummet, but thanks to their free-breeding nature, their population recovers quickly when conditions are more favourable.

Identification: Facial area is mainly yellow with some spots evident. The underparts are light green. Black and yellow barring extends down over the back and there is scalloping over the wings. Tail feathers are bluish-green. Uniquely among psittacines, the budgerigar can be sexed by the colour of its cere, which is blue in cocks and brownish in hens.

AUSTRALIAN PARROTS AND PARAKEETS

Some of the most unusual parrots in the world are found in Australia and New Zealand, such as the ground parrot, which has evolved in the relative absence of predators. In part, the diversity in appearance and lifestyles reflects the harsh environments in which the birds occur, ranging from the searing heat of the Australian desert to the mountainous areas of New Zealand.

Golden-shouldered parakeet

Psephotus chrysopterygius (E)

These beautiful parakeets have a very restricted range, and the entire wild population is made up of no more than around 500 birds. Habitat changes have contributed to their decline, as changes in the grazing patterns of sheep have restricted the availability of grass seeds which form the basis of their diet. Unusually, the golden-shouldered parakeets nest in termite mounds, rather than adopting tree holes like most parrots. They prefer conical-shaped mounds, excavating an entrance which leads via a tunnel to a rounded chamber, around 25cm (10in) in diameter.

Identification: Yellow band on the forehead, with a black cap behind, extending down the back of the head. Greyish mantle and wings. Has an extensive golden yellow area at the shoulder. Sides of the face are bluish-green. The abdomen is orangish-red on a pale yellow background. Hens are mainly yellowish-green, with reddish markings on the abdomen.

Distribution: Four distinct populations are present on the Cape York peninsula in northern Queensland, north-east Australia.
Size: 27cm (11in).
Habitat: Lightly wooded grassland areas.
Nest: Terrestrial termite mounds, hence occasionally known as the ant bed parrot.
Eggs: 5–7, white.
Food: Grass seeds.

Night parrot

Geopsittacus occidentalis (E)

Distribution: Arid central area of Australia. Absent from coastal regions.
Size: 25cm (10in).
Habitat: Arid scrubland near lakes.
Nest: Tunnel lined with sticks within a tussock of spinifex grass.
Eggs: 4–5, white.
Food: Spinifex grass seeds and other vegetation.

These parrots are very hard to observe, thanks to their cryptic coloration, nomadic nature and nocturnal habits. There were suggestions that they had become extinct, but during the 1990s, sightings to the south of Cloncurry confirmed their continued survival. Night parrots are most likely to be encountered among patches of marsh samphire in dried-up lake areas, and in spinifex grass, where they construct a tunnel lined with sticks as a nest site. As their name suggests, night parrots are active after dark when the desert cools down. These birds have few natural predators, but their numbers may have suffered because of introduced mammals such as cats and foxes.

Identification: Mainly green, with a yellower abdomen. Has striations and barring on the body and tail. Similar to the ground parrot (*Pezoporus wallicus*), but a duller green with no red frontal band above the bill. Also has shorter, browner tail feathers. Dark iris. Sexes alike.

Sulphur-crested cockatoo

Cacatua galerita

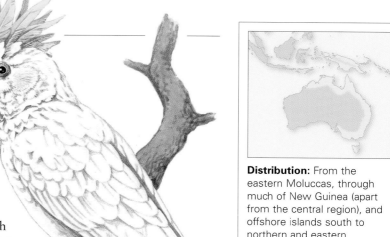

These raucous cockatoos can often be heard
screeching from some distance away as they
fly overhead, particularly in the early morning
and then again towards dusk. They are highly
adaptable and found in a wide range of terrain.
They are not even averse to attacking agricultural
crops, particularly as these are ripening. A close
approach is difficult, especially in areas where they
are persecuted. Several of the flock members watch
for danger while their companions feed, emitting a harsh
alarm call as warning which results in the entire party flying
off. Pairs may often rest in trees during the heat of the day,
and this is when they preen each other.

Identification: Large white body. Has prominent yellow crest
feathers which can be erected if the bird is excited or alarmed.
Tail is relatively short. Some yellowish suffusion under the wings.
Powerful black bill. Greyish-black legs. Has a white eye ring, but
this is pale blue in some races. Iris is black in cock birds and
appears reddish-brown in a good light in hens.

Distribution: From the
eastern Moluccas, through
much of New Guinea (apart
from the central region), and
offshore islands south to
northern and eastern
Australia, the south-eastern
corner, and Tasmania.
Introduced to New Zealand.
Size: 51cm (20in).
Habitat: Open country to
woodland.
Nest: Tree hollow.
Eggs: 2, white.
Food: Seeds, nuts and fruit.

Kea (mountain parrot) (*Nestor notabilis*):
46cm (18in)
Occurs in mountainous areas of North Island,
New Zealand – frequently above the treeline.
Predominantly olive brown, with darker edges to
the individual feathers and a reddish-brown
rump. Dark band on the tail. Elongated black
upper bill. Hens are smaller. Young birds have
yellow not black ceres. Keas have been heavily
persecuted in the past because of their habit of
scavenging on sheep carcasses, gaining these
birds an unjustified reputation as sheep killers.

Galah cockatoo (roseate cockatoo, *Eolophus
roseicapillus*): 38cm (15in)
One of the most common and widely distributed
cockatoos, occurring over virtually the whole of
Australia. Less common on Tasmania, and are
scarce in the Western Desert area. Has grey
upperparts with rose-pink underparts and a
compact, pinkish-white crest. Some variation in
depth of coloration may be apparent, and on rare
occasions, galah cockatoos with white rather
then grey upperparts have been recorded in
flocks. Hens have a reddish-brown iris.

Long-billed corella (*Cacatua tenuirostris*):
41cm (16in)
Found in south-eastern Australia, in the Murray-
Darling area. Predominantly white in colour,
with pronounced pinkish suffusion in the
vicinity of the eyes and on the upper breast.
Blue skin around the eyes. Has a distinctive
long upper bill which is often used for digging
up roots. A yellowish hue can be seen on the
underside of the wings and tail in flight. Has a
short, broad white crest. Sexes are alike.

Ground parrot

Swamp parrot *Pezoporus wallicus*

As their name suggests, ground parrots are
largely terrestrial in their habits, but they
can fly in a zig-zag pattern after being
flushed, and then dip back down into cover.
Their presence is most likely to be revealed
by their whistling calls. These are typically
uttered just before sunrise and at sunset,
although they may be heard during the day.
Cocks croak rather like frogs near the nest,
and this is well concealed with a tunnel-like
entrance on the ground. Their distribution
in heathland areas will suffer when the
ground is swept by fire. Once the diversity
of vegetation has been restored, it is likely
to take four years until pairs start breeding
successfully again.

Identification: Similar to, but more brightly coloured
than the night parrot (*Geopsittacus occidentalis*).
Distinctive wingbar and a long, tapering tail
which can measure up to 20cm (8in) overall.
Red frontal band present in adult birds.
Sexes are alike.

Distribution: Narrow coastal
strips in eastern, south-
eastern and south-western
Australia. Also present on
Tasmania.
Size: 33cm (13.5in).
Habitat: Heathland and
sedge.
Nest: Cup of vegetation on
the ground.
Eggs: 2–6, white.
Food: Seeds and some
invertebrates.

PIGEONS AND DOVES

This group of birds are highly adaptable, as reflected by their reproductive habits. They breed quickly under favourable conditions, often nesting repeatedly in suitable surroundings. This in turn means that they can survive well in fairly inhospitable conditions, such as Australia's arid interior, taking advantage of the unpredictable rains that trigger a resurgence in the plant life.

Diamond dove

Geopelia cuneata

Distribution: Most of Australia, apart from southern and eastern coastal regions.
Size: 20cm (8in).
Habitat: Lightly wooded areas and grassland. Commonly encountered in the outback.
Nest: Loose platform of twigs and vegetation.
Eggs: 2, white.
Food: Mainly small seeds.

These doves live in small parties and usually tolerate quite a close approach, even when walking on the ground. They spend long periods here, seeking seeds and other edible items. When displaying, the cock bird bows in front of the hen and fans his long tail feathers, cooing loudly. The eye ring of the cock becomes more prominent during the breeding season. Pairs tend to be opportunistic breeders, and nest whenever conditions are favourable. In common with many members of this family, incubation duties are shared, with the cock bird sitting for much of the day. The chicks grow rapidly and leave the nest as young as 12 days old, even before they are able to fly well. Diamond doves have been known to spread occasionally outside the usual area of distribution.

Identification: Predominantly greyish brown, with white spots dotted irregularly over the wings. Has chestnut flight feathers. White underside to the tail. Prominent crimson eye ring, especially in cocks during the breeding season. Otherwise sexes alike. Young birds are brownish and lack the white spotting.

Left: The diamond dove's eye ring is a distinctive characteristic.

Crested pigeon

Ocyphaps lophotes

These large pigeons are usually seen in flocks, which may consist of more than 100 individuals, frequently foraging for food on the ground. They have benefited from the spread of agriculture in Australia, not simply because of the increase in crops but also the provision of waterholes for livestock on ranches in more remote areas. Crested pigeons are very adaptable, able to forage for native seeds or cereals and other crops. If disturbed, these pigeons fly up to a nearby tree, often jerking their tails vertically when they land on a branch. They often seek out the protection of a thorn bush or similar shrub when nesting, particularly in the more treeless parts of their range. The colourful areas on the wing form part of the cock bird's display.

Identification: Prominent narrow crest on the top of the head. The underparts are pinkish-grey. The back and wings are brownish and show black barring. Purplish areas are evident towards the rear of the wing. Sexes are similar.

Distribution: Australia, apart from north of the Northern Territory, Cape York peninsula, and the south-east region.
Size: 33cm (13in).
Habitat: Lightly wooded and open areas of country.
Nest: Platform of twigs in a bush.
Eggs: 2, white.
Food: Seeds, other plant matter and invertebrates.

Flock pigeon (harlequin bronzewing, *Phaps histrionica*): 30cm (12in)
Found in northern parts of Australia away from the coastal zone. Highly nomadic by nature. Chestnut mantle, wings, back, tail and lower abdomen. The head is black with a white forehead and a C-shaped marking extending to the cheek from the eye. Also has a white patch on the upper chest and breast. The upper abdomen is greyish. Hen is dark brown. The grey on the throat is surrounded by a white area extending up above the bill. Has greyer underparts.

Squatter pigeon (*Geophaps scripta*): 28cm (11in)
Present in eastern Australia where it ranges north as far as the central area of the Cape York peninsula and south as far as north-eastern New South Wales. Predominantly brown on the upper chest, back and wings with white breast and flanks. Has black and white patterning on the sides of the face. The skin around the eye is red in northern populations. Sexes are alike.

Partridge pigeon (*Geophaps smithii*): 27cm (10.5in)
Found in northern Western Australia, with a separate population in the tip of the Northern Territory. Also present on Melville Island. Mainly brown with a white area extending from the shoulder region and down the sides of the flanks. Some slight barring across the upper breast. Bare area of reddish or orange orbital skin with white area below, bordered by black. Sexes alike.

Red turtle dove

Red collared dove
Streptopelia tranquebarica

These doves are usually spotted in pairs but may also be seen feeding in the company of other related birds such as the laughing dove (*S. senegalensis*) in the east of their range. They tend to feed on the ground, and are especially numerous in agricultural areas where cereals are cultivated. Red turtle doves are not sedentary throughout their range, however, and leave the northerly parts of their range such as Taiwan during the winter months to head further south. Breeding in warmer climates can take place at any stage during the year, although the fragile nature of this dove's nest – a platform of twigs – means that it may sometimes collapse, resulting in the loss of both eggs and chicks.

Identification: Greyish head, becoming darker on the crown, with a prominent black collar across the back of the neck. Underparts are vinous-pink. Wings are brick red. Flight feathers are black and the tail is grey. Hens are brown and more buff-coloured than pink on the underparts. They also have a black collar.

Distribution: Extends across the Indian subcontinent east as far as China and offshore islands, including the Philippines, and south across South-east Asia. Has recently occurred on Java.
Size: 23cm (9in).
Habitat: Open countryside.
Nest: Platform of twigs.
Eggs: 2, whitish.
Food: Seeds.

Distribution: Three distinct populations in northern Australia. Chestnut-bellied form occurs in north-west; the white-bellied form in northern-central region and southern part of Cape York peninsula.
Size: 20cm (8in).
Habitat: Arid areas, where spinifex grass predominates.
Nest: Scrape concealed on the ground.
Eggs: 2, whitish.
Food: Seeds, some invertebrates.

Spinifex pigeon

Plumed rock pigeon *Geophaps plumifera*

Despite inhabiting the arid interior of the Australian continent, these pigeons rarely stray far from water. They favour areas where there are rocky outcrops, often breeding in this terrain and concealing their nest close to a rock. Spinifex pigeons spend much of their time on the ground, where they are encountered much of the time in groups. When they do take to the wing, they fly with their long crest lying back over the neck. If not directly threatened, these pigeons often prefer to run off and only fly away as a last resort. When displaying, cocks will bow and spread their tail feathers in front of a hen. This behaviour is also used as a threatening gesture to other males.

Identification: Rich chestnut, with black barring on the wings and neck area. Long narrow crest on top of the head. Greyish forehead and grey on sides of the face. White area under the throat. Bare reddish skin around the eyes is bordered by black. Whitish area on the belly, depending on the race. Hens may have shorter crests.

EMUS, MALLEE FOWL AND FINCHES

Birds have evolved a number of different breeding strategies, but surely one of the strangest is that of the mallee fowl, whose eggs are hatched entirely by artificial means. This is in distinct contrast to the breeding cycle of the emu, which results in the cock bird remaining constantly with the eggs until they hatch weeks later, often going without food and water for much of this time.

Emu

Dromaius novaehollandiae

These flightless birds are well-adapted for running to escape danger and are capable of sprinting at speeds equivalent to 48kph (30mph) over short distances. They usually walk with little effort at a speed of about 7kph (4mph) and are able to cover more than 2.7m (9ft) in a single stride. When resting, emus lie down on their haunches in the open. They cool themselves by holding out their rudimentary wings, so that heat can be dissipated from the veins flowing close to the skin. After hatching their eggs, the cock rears the chicks on his own, although the group remains together for at least eight months.

Distribution: Most of Australia, apart from desert areas in the interior and some parts of the south-east. Not present on Tasmania.
Size: 190cm (75in).
Habitat: Plains and open woodland areas.
Nest: Scrape on the ground.
Eggs: 5–24, dark green, almost blackish.
Food: Omnivorous.

Identification: Very large. Brownish and shaggy-feathered with long legs and three toes on each foot. Black feathering on the face and down the back of the neck. The sides of the neck are bluish in colour. Has a black bill and reddish eyes. Hens are heavier, weighing up to 55kg (121lb) with deep blue coloration on the face and black feathering on the throat. Young birds have prominently brown-and-white striped backs.

Mallee fowl

Leipoa ocellata

Distribution: Australia. Western coast up to Northern Territory and east to New South Wales.
Size: 60cm (24in).
Habitat: Mallee and other scrubland.
Nest: Mound.
Eggs: 16–33, pinkish.
Food: Omnivorous.

The condition of the soil is very important to mallee fowl, which favour areas of sandy soil that they can excavate easily. Pairs construct a natural incubator for their eggs, in the shape of a massive mound up to 1m (3ft) high and 5m (16ft) in diameter. A hole is dug which is filled with vegetation and left over the winter before being covered with sand. The female then lays her eggs and buries them in the mound where the heat from the decomposing vegetation keeps them warm, at 33°C (91°F). The cock adjusts the temperature by moving the sand. Seven weeks later, the newly hatched chicks dig themselves out.

Identification: Head and neck greyish, with an inconspicuous black crest. Has barred wings, and a blackish line runs down the centre of the breast. Heavily barred upper parts, with brown, black, grey and white markings. Sexes similar but cocks have a booming call and hens crow.

Right: Chicks emerging from the incubation mound.

Zebra finch

Poephila guttata

Living in flocks, these noisy finches are a common sight. Their calls are likened to the sound of toy trumpets. They often perch in the open, on fences, and can be spotted on the ground alongside roads, hopping along and searching for grass seeds. If necessary, they can fly with some agility, catching insects on the wing. Their nest is relatively large and untidy, with extra material often added through the incubation period. Pairs tend to breed repeatedly when conditions are favourable. The nest itself is sited in a variety of localities, ranging from inside the eaves of agricultural buildings to hollow trees.

Identification: Light grey head. Prominent chestnut-orange ear coverts, with a black stripe in front. Has fine zebra-like barring on the chest. The underparts are white and white-spotted chestnut areas extend down the flanks. The back is brownish. The tail is black and white. Hens are much duller, with a brownish-grey head and chest and creamy underparts. Bill is paler than that of the cock and they lack orange ear coverts.

Distribution: Lesser Sunda Islands of Indonesia and most of Australia apart from the far north and the east coast.
Size: 10cm (4in).
Habitat: Scrub, plains, open woodland.
Nest: Made of vegetation.
Eggs: 3–7, pale blue.
Food: Grass seeds and some invertebrates.

Painted firetail (painted finch, *Emblema picta*): 11cm (4.5in)
Extends from western and central parts of Australia to western Queensland. Red face, back, rump and belly. The head, mantle, wings and tip of the tail are brown. Has a black area on the breast and flanks which is broken by white spots. Hens have virtually no red feathering on the underparts and feature a greatly reduced red area on the face.

Star finch (*Neochmia ruficauda*): 10cm (4in)
Widely distributed across northern parts of Australia but is more localized around the Cape York peninsula. Bright red plumage on the sides of the face extends to just behind the eye and down around the throat and is broken by fine white speckling. The breast and flanks are greyish with larger spots. The underparts are whitish. The back and wings are olive-green and the tail is reddish. Hens have a much more restricted area of red on the face, from the bill to the eyes, and are a duller shade overall.

Chestnut-breasted mannikin (chestnut-breasted munia, *Lonchura castaneothorax*): 10cm (4in)
Present on New Guinea and northern and eastern Australia. Also found on some Pacific islands. Has a prominent chestnut area on the breast, with a black border beneath. Underparts are mainly white and there is black barring on the flanks. Undertail coverts are black. There are black areas with paler streaking on the sides of the face, with grey above, and these extend down to the nape. Brown mantle and wings. Golden-yellow rump and tail. Sexes are alike but the hen may be slightly duller in colour.

Spicebird (spotted munia, scaly-breasted munia, *Lonchura punctulata*): 10cm (4in)
Extends from the Indian subcontinent east to China, through South-east Asia and the Malay Peninsula to the Greater Sundas, Sulawesi and other islands. Introduced in some areas. Head and upperparts are rich brown, with black or dark brown crescent-shaped patterning on the white of the underparts. Spotted rump and yellowish tail. Sexes are alike.

Gouldian finch

Chloebia gouldiae

The gouldian ranks as one of the most stunningly-coloured finches in the world. Unfortunately, its numbers are in a severe decline. This appears to be at least in part due to a tiny parasite which spreads to nestlings via their parents and invades their airways. This leads to severe breathing difficulty and, frequently, premature death. The head coloration of this finch naturally varies – most often it is black or deep red, while, less commonly, it is an orangish yellow. These are not separate subspecies, but rather they are naturally occurring colour variants within a flock due to free interbreeding among these colourful birds.

Identification: The colour of the head is variable but the rest of the finch's body is consistent in colour. Has a bright blue collar around the head. Mantle and wings are green. Has a purple area on the breast. The underparts are yellow and the rump is blue. Pointed tail. Hens are duller with a shorter tail.

Distribution: Northern parts of Australia.
Size: 13.5cm (5in).
Habitat: Grassy plains with some trees.
Nest: Ball-like, often located in a hollow tree.
Eggs: 4–8, white.
Food: Mainly grass seeds and some invertebrates.

BIRDS OF PREY

Keen vision, fast flight and agility allow many birds of prey to hunt effectively, but those that feed primarily on carrion, in the form of dead animals, require a different strategy, as exemplified by vultures. While acute vision is also vital for them, they need to stay airborne with minimum effort, covering large distances while searching for the carcass of a large herbivore on the ground below.

Little falcon

Australian hobby *Falco longipennis*

These small, adaptable falcons may be seen flying during the day, and through into the night, particularly where there are artificial lights which attract insects, moths and similar invertebrates after dark. They catch their prey in flight, and are agile enough to take fast-flying quarry such as swallows. Farmers often welcome their presence because they feed on sparrows. Little falcons will build their nest in a tree, although other less conventional sites such as electricity poles may sometimes be used, especially in areas where alternatives are not readily available. After nesting, hens, especially, migrate north, leaving Australia for the winter. Populations elsewhere, in the Lesser Sundas for example, are sedentary.

Above: Little falcons have long, narrow wings, which helps their agility when hunting other birds.

Identification: Brown forehead, becoming blackish on the sides of the face with a white area from the throat up the sides of the neck. Streaked white on the breast, becoming rufous on the underparts. Wings are slate-grey with lighter edging. Barred tail has a white tip. Hens larger.

Distribution: Australia including Tasmania, ranging to New Guinea, New Britain and the Moluccas outside the breeding period. Also occurs on the Lesser Sundas.
Size: 35cm (14in).
Habitat: Open and wooded areas.
Nest: Platform made of sticks.
Eggs: 2–4, white with reddish-brown markings.
Food: Small birds, bats and invertebrates.

Grey-faced buzzard

Frog hawk *Butastur indicus*

These buzzards are frequently seen in areas close to water, where they hunt amphibians, which form a significant part of their diet. The grey-faced buzzard seeks a good vantage point and then uses its keen eyesight to pinpoint its prey before swooping down to seize it. These birds come together to form massive flocks, which may number thousands of birds when on migration. The migration routes may stretch along the Pacific coastline of Japan to the Philippines, with a separate route via Korea on the Asiatic mainland.
When migrating in such numbers, grey-faced buzzards are vulnerable to being shot by hunters, and certainly in some areas, they are declining in numbers because of this threat.

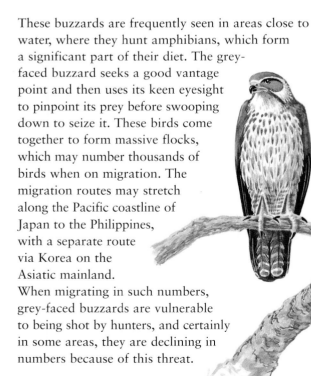

Identification: White throat, broken by a black central area, with a white stripe above the eyes. Has a greyish-brown head and brown back and chest. The underparts are white with much brown barring. The tail is brown with black barring. Has long wings. Yellow legs and feet. Young birds less colourful. Sexes alike.

Distribution: Eastern Asia, Japan and the Philippines. Widely distributed through South-east Asia, down across the Malay Peninsula to the Greater Sundas, Sulawesi and neighbouring islands.
Size: 46cm (18in).
Habitat: Open country with nearby wooded areas.
Nest: Small platform of twigs in a tree.
Eggs: 2–4, white.
Food: Frogs, reptiles and rodents.

Himalayan griffon vulture

Gyps himalayensis

These massive vultures glide almost effortlessly over long distances, relying primarily on their keen eyesight to locate the carcasses of large herbivores and other creatures on the ground. The size of this vulture means that it can drive off other smaller relatives at feeding sites, with the exception of the more assertive Eurasian black vulture (*Aegypius monachus*). Large numbers are drawn to a suitable feeding site, where they rip the flesh off the carcass quickly and efficiently using their powerful hooked bills. Their largely bald heads mean they can feed without their plumage becoming matted with blood.

Identification: Variable, whitish-buff. Bare purplish-pink skin at the base of the neck. Greyish face. Wings and tail dark brown. Sexes alike. Young birds are darker in colour than adults.

Distribution: Himalayan region, from Pakistan to western and central parts of China.
Size: 115–150cm (45–59in).
Habitat: Mountainous regions, from 900–5,000m (3,000–16,500ft).
Nest: Sticks on cliff-face.
Eggs: 1, white with traces of red markings.
Food: Carrion.

Black falcon (*Falco subniger*): 56cm (22in)
Found in central and eastern Australia. Black with light edging on back and wing feathers and a white tip to the tail. Black bill and cere. Looks broad-winged in flight. Hens are larger.

Spotted harrier (*Circus assimilis*): 61cm (24in)
Present on Sulawesi, the Sula Islands, and mainland Australia. Has white spotting on the underparts and pale grey markings over the wings. Chestnut face, with greyish collar. The tail is barred. Hens are larger.

Black-breasted kite (black-breasted buzzard, *Hamirostra melanosternon*): 61cm (24in)
Found in northern and western areas of Australia. Blackish crown, face, breast and back. Chestnut-orange plumage on the back of the head and neck and on the underparts. White areas on the wings. Dark tail. Powerful, greyish bill with dark tip. Hens are larger.

Long-billed vulture (*Gyps indicus*): 80-100cm (32-39in)
Ranges from south-eastern Pakistan and all India (apart from the extreme south) into Indo-China and the northern Malay Peninsula. Has a bare greyish head with white plumage at the base of the neck. The wings are brown, but become blackish on the flight feathers and tail. Underparts are buff-brown. The bill is more slender than in related species. Sexes are alike.

Swamp harrier

Western marsh-harrier *Circus aeruginosus*

Unlike many birds of prey, this harrier is a truly opportunistic hunter. It raids the nests of other birds, as well as catching the birds themselves, and also hunts mammals, such as rabbits, by swooping on them in the open. Its food varies, partly depending on its range, and may change throughout the year. During the winter, even the carcasses of dead whales washed ashore in coastal areas may feature in its diet. In Asia, these birds tend to migrate southwards at this time of year. Pairs regularly return to the same nest site in the following spring.

Identification: Plumage varies according to the race. Head is brownish with white streaks. Darker streaking on a buff chest. The abdomen is entirely brown. Wings are brown with rufous edging to the feathers. White and grey areas are also apparent. Tail is pale greyish. Hens are larger, with a yellowish-cream suffusion on the head, throat and shoulder. Young birds resemble hens but have darker shoulder markings.

Distribution: Extensive, being found in Africa and Europe as well as western Asia, where one population is centred across the entire Indian subcontinent and Sri Lanka. Further north, the species extends from Asia Minor eastwards to Mongolia.
Size: 48–56 cm (19–22in).
Habitat: Marshland and nearby open country.
Nest: Pile of reeds in a secluded reedbed.
Eggs: 2–7, pale bluish-white.
Food: Birds, plus other small vertebrates.

NECTAR-FEEDERS AND SEED-EATERS

Within the parrot family, some members of the group feed mainly on seeds, whereas others such as the lorikeets rely on their specially adapted tongues to feed on nectar. Small birds, notably sunbirds, also feed on nectar, but use their long, narrow bills to reach it. While this restricts their distribution largely to the tropics, other species such as pigeons and doves have more adaptable feeding habits.

Crimson rosella

Pennant's parakeet *Platycercus*

Inhabiting a variety of localities, these colourful parakeets can become really quite tame. Although they prefer to feed on the ground, they will take food such as seed placed on bird tables readily and visit gardens on a regular basis. Their presence there is not always welcomed, however, as they may also strip off branches and eat blossoms, attacking fruit crops as well on occasion. The immature plumage is surprisingly variable, with birds from northern areas tending to have more red plumage than those in southern populations, which are mainly green on fledging. It takes the crimson rosella up to 15 months to attain its adult plumage.

Identification: Crimson head and underparts. Has black scalloped patterning over the wings. Prominent blue cheek patches. Has blue on the edge of the wings as well as on the tail. Sexes alike. Young birds are often predominantly green on fledging.

Distribution: Two distinct populations in coastal parts of eastern and south-eastern Australia. Introduced to New Zealand.
Size: 37cm (15in).
Habitat: Woodland, farmland and gardens.
Nest: Tree hollow.
Eggs: 5–8, white.
Food: Seeds and other plant matter.

Rainbow lorikeet

Trichoglossus haematodus

There is considerable diversity in the appearance of these lorikeets, and approximately 21 different races have been identified over the islands where they occur. The variation is mainly in the colour of the neck and breast plumage, giving rise to local names such as the green-naped lorikeet (*T. h. haematodus*). Rainbow lorikeets are conspicuous, noisy birds with bold natures. In some parts of eastern Australia, wild flocks regularly visit campsites, where they are a major tourist attraction, feeding on trays of sponge cake soaked in honey water held up for them by visitors. They are more active during the early morning and late afternoon and tend to roost quietly when the sun is at its hottest.

Above: The tip of the rainbow lorikeet's tongue is covered with tiny papillae, which effectively sweep up the pollen grain as it feeds on flowers.

Identification: Dark bluish head and green back and wings. Often has barring on the underparts. Breast is yellow to red, with a variable amount of scalloping. Collar varies from green through yellow to red, depending on the individual. Sexes are alike.

Distribution: Islands from Bali eastwards through the Moluccas and New Guinea to the Solomon Islands and New Caledonia. Occurs in Australia south from the Cape York Peninsula along the east, south-east and south coasts to the Eyre Peninsula. They also move between islands.
Size: 26cm (10in).
Habitat: Woodland, farmland and gardens.
Nest: Tree hollow.
Eggs: 2–3, white.
Food: Nectar, pollen, fruit and some seeds.

Spotted turtle dove (*Streptopelia chinensis*):
31cm (12¹/₂in)
Wide distribution from eastern Afghanistan across southern parts of Asia to China and offshore islands. South through the Malay Peninsula to the Sundas and the Philippines. Introduced to numerous areas, including parts of Australia and New Zealand. Has a distinctive black neck patch that is spotted with white markings. Greyish head. Has pinkish-buff underparts. The wings, back and tail are a brownish shade, often with darker markings apparent. Sexes alike.

Bar-shouldered dove (*Geopelia humeralis*):
29cm (11¹/₂in)
Northern and eastern parts of Australia and southern New Guinea. Has a copper-coloured patch on the neck and black barring over much of the brown upperparts. The forehead and sides of the face, as well as the breast, are greyish. The underparts are predominantly pink-buff. Sexes alike.

Black-capped white-eye (*Zosterops atricapilla*):
11cm (4¹/₂in)
Extends through the Malay Peninsula to Sumatra and Borneo. Has distinctive blackish feathering on the front and sides of the face and a white eye ring. The upperparts are olive green. The underparts are yellowish with grey flanks. The tail is also dark. Sexes alike.

Purple-throated sunbird (*Nectarinia sperata*):
14cm (5¹/₂in)
Extends from eastern Pakistan, mainly through coastal parts of South-east Asia, east to the Philippines then south to the Sunda islands and Sulawesi. Cocks may appear almost entirely black but have a purplish throat with crimson on the belly and upper abdomen. Hens have a characteristic greenish-yellow belly and undertail coverts, with dark olive upperparts and a black tail.

Oriental white-eye

Zosterops palpebrosa

The relatively narrow yet stocky and slightly curved bill of this bird is used not only to probe flowers for nectar, but also to grab invertebrates. The bill is not especially powerful, however, and this results in oriental white-eyes tending to stab at fruit rather than biting off chunks. White-eyes are seen in loose flocks, often foraging through vegetation in the company of other birds. These birds are very active and extremely agile and can be observed hopping from branch to branch. They call frequently to other members of the group, with their calls consisting of a series of twittering notes, combined when necessary with sharper alarm calls. When breeding, pairs of these birds build compact, well-constructed nests that are usually hidden and supported in the fork of a tree.

Distribution: From northern India eastwards to southern China. Present across South-east Asia and the Malay Peninsula to the Greater Sunda islands.
Size: 11cm (4¹/₂in).
Habitat: Vegetation in lowland areas.
Nest: Cup-shaped in vegetation.
Eggs: 2, pale blue.
Food: Invertebrates, nectar and fruit.

Identification: Yellowish-green upperparts with a characteristic narrow, white ring of plumage around the eyes. Underparts may be entirely yellow or the flanks may be greyish, depending on the subspecies. Sexes are alike.

Yellow-breasted sunbird

Olive-backed sunbird *Nectarinia jugularis*

Although sunbirds are quite common on mainland Asia, the yellow-breasted variety is the only species present on Australia. They use their long bills to obtain nectar from plants, and also hunt invertebrates, with spiders being a favoured food. In spite of its small size, the yellow-breasted sunbird is quite bold, even to the extent of siting its nests under the roofs of verandas and porches and in the vicinity of other outbuildings. It uses the gossamer threads of spiders' webs rather like cotton to bind the nest fibres together, frequently incorporating a trailing tail beneath as part of the design. The internal area of the nest is lined with softer materials such as down feathers. The young in the nest are reared almost exclusively on insects.

Identification: Brownish-green upperparts and bright yellow underparts. Adult cocks easily identified by a dark purplish metallic area on the throat, which is more extensive in breeding plumage. Narrow black bill. Short tail. Young birds resemble adult hens.

Distribution: From China across South-east Asia and the Malay Peninsula to parts of Indonesia and New Guinea. Extends south to north-eastern coastal region of Australia.
Size: 11cm (4¹/₂in).
Habitat: Areas where there are trees in the vicinity.
Nest: Pendulous, made of vegetation.
Eggs: 2–3, grey-green with mottling.
Food: Nectar, invertebrates.

HONEYEATERS, FAIRY WRENS AND OTHER AUSTRALASIAN SPECIES

There is a clear divide between birds found in Australia and New Guinea, and those occurring on the mainland of Asia and the Greater Sunda chain of islands. This division in distribution was first identified by the Victorian zoologist William Wallace, after whom the Wallace line is named, which marks the border between the Asiatic and Australasian zones. This border runs between the islands of Bali and Lombok.

Plain honeyeater

Nondescript honeyeater *Pycnopygius ixoides*

Its drab plumage means that the plain honeyeater is easily overlooked, especially when it occurs in the company of other related species. It is quiet by nature, which presents a further difficulty in assessing its numbers with any accuracy. Some ornithologists suggest that these honeyeaters are quite rare, although others think that they are in fact quite common but are not easily observed. When these honeyeaters feeds on flowers that produce large amounts of pollen, the pollen may stain their heads temporarily, giving them a yellowish hue. Honeyeaters as a group have a very important role in pollinating flowers as they feed, not just from pollen transferred on their heads, but also from pollen on their brush-like tongue.

Identification: Corresponds well to the name of nondescript honeyeater, in that its plumage is plain, drab brown with no instantly recognizable features, apart from a greyer tone to the plumage on the head. Its bill is quite small compared with related species. Brown irises. Sexes alike.

Distribution: All of New Guinea, apart from the southern Trans-fly region.
Size: 18cm (7in).
Habitat: Lowland areas, but has been known to extend up into the hills.
Nest: Cup-shaped.
Eggs: 2, pinkish with darker spotting.
Food: Fruit, nectar and invertebrates.

Little wattlebird

Brush mockingbird *Anthochaera chrysoptera*

In spite of its name, and unlike its close relative the red wattlebird (*A. carunculata*), this species has no fleshy swellings, or wattle, on its neck. The heavily streaked plumage on the little wattlebird's body helps to conceal its presence well when it is seeking food among its favourite shrub, the banksia. Little wattlebirds tend to be rather bold by nature, especially in areas such as gardens, and will allow a relatively close approach. They are also quite noisy and have a varied repertoire of calls. They raise their tails when they are excited, and will rattle their bills without actually giving voice. Their nest is concealed in a shrub and is usually lined with a soft material such as loose bark stripped from eucalyptus trees.

Identification: Heavily streaked plumage with lighter underparts. The silvery streaking is most apparent on the sides of the head and neck. Rufous patches on the wings are apparent in flight. White tip to the relatively long tail feathers. Black pointed bill. Sexes alike.

Distribution: South-western and south-eastern parts of mainland Australia. Also present on Tasmania.
Size: 30cm (12in).
Habitat: Woodlands, parks and gardens.
Nest: Cup-shaped, made of twigs.
Eggs: 1–2, salmon-pink with darker reddish spots.
Food: Invertebrates, fruit and nectar.

Left: Invertebrates feature prominently in the diet of young little wattlebirds.

Superb blue wren

Malurus cyaneus

Despite their small size, superb blue wrens are notoriously aggressive and territorial when nesting, even to the point of both sexes attacking their reflections in a window or a car hubcap parked by a verge. After the breeding period, the family stays together, although hens leave the group in the spring. Young cocks remain and help to feed the first round of chicks in the following year, and this allows the adults to build a new nest and breed again very quickly. These blue wrens have adapted well to garden life, searching out invertebrates in the plants.

Identification: Cock bird in breeding plumage has a bright blue head, extending back along the sides of the neck to the mantle. Has a blackish intervening area. Breast is a characteristic bluish-black, with whitish underparts. Long, dark blue tail. Wings brownish. Hen is brown with a whitish throat, while the underparts are fawn-white in colour. Tail is brown with a bluish wash. Reddish-brown feathers around the eye and similar-coloured bill distinguish hens from out-of-colour cock birds, whose bills are black.

Distribution: Eastern and south-eastern Australia, including Tasmania.
Size: 14cm (5½in).
Habitat: Dense, low vegetation.
Nest: Domed structure made of plant fibres.
Eggs: 3–4, pinkish-white.
Food: Mostly small invertebrates.

Noisy friarbird (*Philemon corniculatus*): 35cm (14in)
Found down the eastern side of Australia, although not in the extreme north or the far south. Brownish back, wings and tail with a ruff of creamy feathers around the neck and long silvery plumes on the upper part of the breast. Underparts greyish-white. Head bare and black with a swelling on the upper bill close to the base. White tips to the tail prominent in flight. Sexes alike.

Striated pardalote (*Pardalotus striatus*): 11.5cm (4½in)
Present in various forms through much of Australia including Tasmania and other islands. Variable appearance, depending on race. Blackish crown with white markings. Greyish back with pale orange to red streak above the eyes. Grey and yellow evident on the underparts. Short blackish tail. White edging to the flight feathers. Hens are duller in overall coloration.

Figbird (banana bird, *Sphecotheres viridis*): 30cm (12in)
Present on the eastern Lesser Sundas, New Guinea, Kai Islands and others in the Torres Strait south to Australia, being present in the north and eastern coastal areas as far as New South Wales. Has black plumage over much of the head, and bare area of red skin around the eyes. Green wing and rump, with black tail. Underparts vary from green to yellow, depending on the race. Whiter around the vent region. Hens have speckled underparts with brown or greenish back, wings and tail.

Pallid cuckoo (*Cuculus pallidus*): 33cm (13½in)
Found over much of Australia, including Tasmania. Undertakes seasonal movements and is occasionally seen in the Moluccas and New Guinea over the winter. Has a dark area around the eyes, a white area on the nape and white markings on the wings and flight feathers. The underparts are relatively pale. The long tail has whitish edging. Sexes are alike.

Flame robin

Bank robin *Petroica phoenicea*

These birds are unusual among the many robins found in Australia and Tasmania, simply because they form flocks outside the breeding season, with hens usually predominating in these groups. When nesting, these birds occur in wooded areas, before moving into more open countryside for the rest of the year. Although the flame robins are more conspicuous in the open, the hens' dull-coloured plumage means that it can prove difficult to identify them correctly. The site chosen for the cup-shaped nest is variable, ranging from a fork in a tree to a cavity in the trunk, and may even be situated beneath a rocky overhang. The construction process usually takes at least two weeks. The nest is bound using the thread from a spider's web.

Distribution: South-eastern Australia including Tasmania
Size: 14cm (5½in).
Habitat: Wooded and open country.
Nest: Bulky, cup-shaped.
Eggs: 3–4, greenish-white with dark markings.
Food: Invertebrates.

Identification: The head, wings and tail are dark grey apart from a prominent white area above the bill and white wing patches. Throat area is brownish too. Has buff and white markings across the wings and orange-red underparts. Hens have greyish-brown upperparts and white underparts.

STARLINGS, MYNAHS, SPIDERHUNTERS AND LAUGHING THRUSHES

The starling family Sturnidae is well represented both in Asia and Australia, where the European starling (Sturnus vulgaris) has been introduced alongside native species. Mynahs are a distinct grouping within the starling family, with this description being applied to large, short-tailed species with iridescent black plumage. Laughing thrushes, however, are found only in Asia, and have an attractive song in many cases.

Singing starling

Aplonis cantoroides

Distribution: New Guinea and neighbouring islands extending to the Bismarck Archipelago and the Solomon Islands.
Size: 19cm (7¹/₂in).
Habitat: Mainly open country.
Nest: Cavity in a tree hole or elsewhere.
Eggs: 2–3, pale blue with brown and violet spotting.
Food: Mainly fruit but also eats invertebrates.

During the breeding season, singing starlings are likely to be observed in pairs or even singly, but after the chicks have fledged, they join up to form large flocks comprised of both adult and juvenile birds. Perhaps surprisingly, in spite of their name, singing starlings are not talented songsters, although their calls are less harsh than those of many starlings. These starlings are seen predominantly in coastal lowland areas, and are a common sight in towns there. They have even been known to nest in buildings on occasions.

Identification: Predominantly black in colour with a marked green-metallic iridescence, depending on the light. Plumage on the back of the head and neck is elongated, forming hackles. The square, short tail is blackish. Iris is a bright contrasting orange-red. Bill and legs are black. Sexes alike. Young birds very different, having brown wings with some greenish suffusion, while the underparts are whitish with brown streaking. Iris brown.

Yellow-faced mynah

Papuan mynah *Mino dumontii*

Studies have revealed how these mynahs have different dialects in parts of their range. Those living in the vicinity of New Guinea's main town – Port Moresby – have call notes consisting primarily of two syllables, whereas in mynahs living elsewhere through their range, three or more distinct notes running together can be identified. Yellow-faced mynahs are believed to pair for life, even though they may congregate in large flocks comprised of hundreds of individuals at times. When nesting, a pair may be assisted by members of their previous brood. Once the chicks have hatched, insects and even small vertebrates assume greater importance in their diet to provide protein.

Identification: Stocky in stature. Predominantly glossy black. White rump and undertail coverts, and a white wing bar too. Large area of bright orange skin encircling the eyes, with an orange throat and an orange area on the abdomen as well. Yellow bill and legs. Sexes alike. The orange facial skin is paler in young birds.

Distribution: New Guinea, apart from the mountainous central zone, and adjoining islands.
Size: 26cm (10¹/₂in).
Habitat: In or near wooded areas.
Nest: Tree hole.
Eggs: 1–2, light blue with dark markings.
Food: Fruit and invertebrates.

Common mynah

House mynah *Acridotheres tristis*

Distribution: Extends from south-eastern Iran and Afghanistan across central and southern Asia. Range is extending in some areas and the common mynah has been introduced to many islands around the world from Madagascar to Hawaii, Australia and New Zealand
Size: 25cm (10in)
Habitat: Open country.
Nest: Usually built in a cavity
Eggs: 2–6, bluish
Food: Fruit, invertebrates

As their name suggests, these mynahs are a common sight through much of their range, in agricultural areas as well as in towns and cities. They are very adaptable and this is reflected in their choice of nest sites. Common mynahs have been recorded breeding in lamp posts, under the eaves of houses, in old machinery and even in air-conditioning units. An equally wide range of materials, from grass and leaves to pieces of plastic and paper, may be used in the construction. Common mynahs are often seen in pairs, frequently foraging on the ground in parks and gardens for invertebrates. This is one of just a few avian species that have actively benefited from changes in the landscape arising from human development.

Identification: Black head with broad yellowish bare patch of skin around the eyes. Wings and body brownish with a white patch on the wings, white undertail coverts and a white tip to the tail. Yellow bill. Sexes alike.

Chestnut-cheeked starling (violet-backed starling, *Sturnia philippensis*): 18cm (7in) Breeding grounds are centred in northern and central parts of Japan, with overwintering occurring further south, in Borneo, southern Sulu islands, parts of the Philippines and elsewhere, although the exact range has yet to be defined. Rarely seen on the Asiatic mainland in China. Cock bird has pale chestnut-coloured patches on the cheeks, greyish underparts, white wing bar and violet back. Hens by comparison are brownish-grey overall with paler underparts. A wing bar is also apparent.

Crested mynah (Chinese jungle mynah, *Acridotheres cristatellus*): 26cm (10 1/2 in) Occurs in central and south-eastern China, extending to northern Indo-China. Also occurs on Hainan and Taiwan, and sometimes seen in western parts of Japan. Black, with a low crest extending back from the bill towards the eyes. Distinctive ivory bill. White patch on the wing and yellow iris. Sexes alike.

Hwamei (melodious laughing thrush, *Garrulax canorus*) : 21.5cm (8 1/2 in) Occurs in northern Indo-China and southern parts of China, including Hong Kong, as well as Hainan and Taiwan. Predominantly brown, with darker wings and tail. The tail is barred. Has dark streaking on the head and breast. The white plumage around the eye extends back to form a stripe running down each side of the neck. Has a "hwamei", which translates as "beautiful eyebrow". Sexes alike.

Spectacled spiderhunter

Greater yellow-eared spiderhunter *Arachnothera flavigaster*

Distribution: Extends from western Myanmar (Burma) through southern Thailand and the Malay Peninsula to Sumatra, Java and Borneo.
Size: 21cm (8in)
Habitat: Open forests and scrub.
Nest: Suspended structure.
Eggs: 2–3, pinkish with dark markings.
Food: Invertebrates, nectar.

Flowers that are red or orange in colour and shaped like trumpets tend to attract these nectar-feeding birds, which are members of the sunbird family in spite of the lack of iridescence in their plumage. They can be very aggressive, particularly during the breeding season, with an established cock bird chasing rivals away without any hesitation. At this time, the long, pointed bill of these birds is used rather like a needle to sew the nest in place, using gossamer threads of spiders' webs for this purpose. Spiderhunters are very bold birds by nature, and can often be seen in the open, particularly during the morning and later part of the afternoon, searching for food.

Identification: Relatively large spiderhunter. Predominantly olive green, darker in colour on the head, back and wings. There is a yellow suffusion to the plumage of the underparts. Yellow circles resembling spectacles encircle the eyes, and there are adjoining yellow ear patches. Narrow, long, down-curving black bill. Sexes alike.

BULBULS AND OTHER GARDEN BIRDS

There is a wide range of birds that may be encountered in garden surroundings, and they can be quite bold in this type of environment. A number are valuable allies of people, catching invertebrates that would otherwise become pests, particularly in tropical areas, although they also inflict damage on crops in some regions, especially when these are maturing.

Red-whiskered bulbul

Pycnonotus jocusus

These lively bulbuls are quite conspicuous through their range, occurring in small groups. They sing for quite long periods from the same perch, especially at the start of the breeding season, although the crest may not always be clearly visible at this stage. Sometimes they may be seen on branches but they will also perch on telephone cables in the open. Red-whiskered bulbuls are rarely seen on the ground, preferring to seek their food in trees. They are also sufficiently agile to be able to catch invertebrates in flight. When breeding, their nest is typically constructed up to 3m (10ft) off the ground in a bush or tree, being made of plant matter and lined with smaller plant fibres.

Identification: Head black, with a tall crest extending back towards the rear. Red patch behind the eyes, with white cheeks and throat broken by thin black lines. The wings and back are brownish. The underparts are buff in colour, apart from the vent area, which is red. Sexes alike.

Distribution: Extends from India eastwards to China and South-east Asia. Introduced in various localities including Australia.
Size: 20cm (8in).
Habitat: Open wooded areas and villages.
Nest: Cup-shaped, made of vegetation.
Eggs: 2–4, pinkish white with darker markings.
Food: Fruit and invertebrates.

Edible-nest swiftlet

Collocalia unicolor

Distribution: Found on many offshore islands, including the Andamans, Nicobars and the Sundas. Also present on parts of the South-east Asian mainland at lower altitudes, including Myanmar (Burma), Thailand and the Malay Peninsula.
Size: 13cm (5in).
Habitat: Scrubland and towns.
Nest: Made entirely of saliva.
Eggs: 2, white.
Food: Invertebrates.

Although they fly in daylight, edible-nest swiftlets also rely on echolocation, rather like bats, which enables them to fly around caves in darkness. The rattling sounds that they utter reverberate off nearby objects, allowing them to fly without hitting any obstructions. The nests made by these swiftlets are constructed from saliva, and are traditionally harvested as the key ingredient of birds' nest soup. Over-collection of these nests and the resulting disruption of long-standing breeding colonies has led to a decline in the populations of edible-nest swiftlets at a number of localities through their range.

Identification: Upperparts blackish-brown, with brown underparts. Rump colour is variable, depending on the distribution. It is palest, bordering on white, in the case of birds originating from Singapore, and much darker in those found further north.

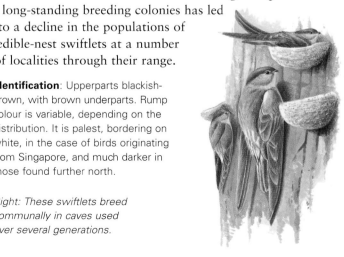

Right: These swiftlets breed communally in caves used over several generations.

Straw-headed bulbul (yellow-crowned bulbul, *Pycnonotus zeylanicus*): 28cm (11in)
Extends through the Malay Peninsula down to the Greater Sunda islands. This is one of the larger bulbuls. It has a straw-yellow head and a white throat. Black lines run through the eyes and extend backwards from the side of the bill. Has a greyish chest with white streaking. This becomes grey on the belly and has a yellow vent. Olive-brown back, with whitish streaking near the neck. Sexes alike.

Collared finchbill (*Spizixos semitorques*): 23cm (9in)
Found in central, eastern and southern parts of China and Taiwan. Has olive-green upperparts with the underparts a more golden-olive shade. The bill is short and thick and less pointed than in other bulbuls. Has a low, rounded crest on a black head. Has white streaking on the sides of the face, white lores and a white collar. The tail has a black tip. Sexes alike.

House crow (Indian crow, *Corvus splendens*): 43cm (17in)
Occurs mainly in Asia from India eastwards to the western parts of South-east Asia, but also present in localities in the Middle East and Africa. Lighter greyish neck, back and underparts than other crows but with a jet black face, crown and throat. Sexes alike.

Coppersmith barbet

Crimson-breasted barbet *Megalaima haemacephala*

The monotonous, repetitive calls of the coppersmith barbet resemble the sound of hammering on metal, which accounts for its unusual name. Their calls can be repeated as frequently as 100 times or more per minute, and this behaviour has led to them becoming known less flatteringly as "brainfever birds". They can also use their stout bills just like a hammer to tap away at rotten wood to create a suitable nesting cavity, which may be used for roosting purposes as well. In common with other barbets, the coppersmith displays the characteristic outward-curving longer feathers around the base of its bill, which are responsible for the common name of this group of birds ("barbet" actually means "bearded").

Distribution: Ranges from western Pakistan across Asia to south-western China, and through the Malay Peninsula to Sumatra and Java. Occurs on some Philippine islands.
Size: 15cm (6in).
Habitat: Wooded areas, often in cities and gardens.
Nest: Tree cavity.
Egg: 2–3, white.
Food: Fruit and invertebrates.

Identification: Red area above stocky, dark bill and across the breast, separated by pale yellow, which is also present above and below the eyes. Crown and lower part of the cheeks are black. Lower underparts light greyish with dark green streaks, while the upperparts are olive green. Legs reddish. Sexes alike.

Java sparrow

Rice bird *Lonchura oryzivora*

These members of the munia group are drawn to areas where cereals are ripening and flocks can inflict considerable damage on rice crops at this stage, especially when they descend in large numbers. Java sparrows are quite conspicuous finches, thanks to their large size and unusual coloration. Groups often settle in the evening on top of buildings before heading to their roosting sites. They frequently engage in a behaviour known as "clumping" when resting for any length of time, with the birds perching against each other. Pairs may nest under the eaves of buildings, although often they will use tree cavities for this purpose.

Identification: Black head with white cheek patches, grey chest and back with pinkish belly and white undertail coverts. Rump and tail above are black. Prominent reddish ring around the eyes. The large bill is pinkish. Both the eye ring and the bill may appear slightly enlarged in cock birds during the breeding season. Sexes are otherwise alike.

Distribution: Naturally found on Bali, Java and Kangean (part of the Greater Sunda islands) but introduced elsewhere both in the region – on Lombok, for example – and further afield in Venezuela and Puerto Rico, among other localities.
Size: 13cm (5in).
Habitat: Cultivated grasslands and gardens.
Nest: Domed nest with side entrance.
Eggs: 3–8, white.
Food: Cereal seeds such as rice, plus invertebrates.

GLOSSARY

The forest, or Tasmanian, raven (Corvus tasmanicus), a member of the Corvidae family.

avifauna: The birds of a specified region or period of time.

breeding plumage: The often brightly coloured plumage that the cock birds of some species adopt before breeding.

carpal: The area of plumage at the top of the leading edge of the wings.

cere: The fleshy area encompassing the nostrils located above the bill. Often especially prominent in parrots.

cline: A gradual change in a characteristic of a species, such as size, or the frequency of a characteristic, over a geographical area.

columbiforms: The group of birds that comprises doves and pigeons.

contour feathers: The smaller feathers covering the head and body.

corvid: A member of the Corvidae family, such as crows, ravens and jays.

coverts: The specific contour feathers covering the wings and base of the tail.

cryptic: Refers to coloration or formation that conceals or camouflages.

culmen: The central ridge of the bill.

down: Plumage of a loose texture that primarily serves to conserve body heat.

eclipse plumage: A transitional plumage seen, for example, in the drakes of some ducks, occurring after they have moulted their breeding plumage.

frugivore: A species that eats mainly fruit.

irruption: An unpredictable movement of large numbers of birds outside their normal range.

lek: An area where the male birds of certain species gather to perform courtship displays.

lores: The area between the bill and the eyes on each side of the face.

mantle: Plumage of the same colour occurring on the back and folded wings of certain birds.

melanistic: A dominance of black pigment in the plumage, often in a particular colour phase.

migrant: A bird that undertakes regular seasonal movements, breeding in one locality and overwintering in another.

nidicolous: Refers to the chicks of species that remain in the nest for some time after hatching.

nidifugous: Describes the chicks of species that leave the nest immediately after hatching.

nuchal: The plumage at the nape of the neck.

orbital: The skin around the eye.

pectoral: Of or located on the breast.

precocial: Refers to newly hatched young that are covered with down and fully active.

race: A geographically isolated population below the level of species, which differs slightly, typically in size or colour, from other races of the same species.

raptor: A bird of prey that actively hunts its food.

ratite: Any of the large, flightless birds, such as the emu (*Dromaius novaehollandiae*), that have a flat breastbone without the keel-like ridge of flying birds.

scapular: Of or on the shoulder.

spatule: Spoon-shaped or spatula-shaped feathers, on the wing or the tail.

speculum: A distinctive patch of colour evident in the flight feathers of certain birds, particularly ducks and parrots.

syrinx: The voice organ of birds, located at the base of the trachea (windpipe).

tarsal: Refers to the area at or below the ankle in birds, as in tarsal spur.

torpidity: A state of dormancy, usually undertaken to conserve energy and combat possible starvation in the face of adverse environmental conditions.

wattle: A wrinkled, fleshy piece of skin hanging from the throat or chin of some birds, or present on the head.

zygodactyl: The 2:2 perching grip, with two toes holding the perch at the front and two at the back.

INDEX